DO YOU:
- Panic before you board an airplane?
- Freak out before a presentation?
- Hyperventilate when you have to leave the house?
- Get the shakes before a date?
- Want to scream when you enter an elevator?
- Feel your stomach drop when the boss wants to see you?
- Smoke too many cigarettes?
- Stay up all night tossing and turning?
- Drink too much coffee?
- Obsess about people, things and places?

You don't have to suffer from anxiety and panic attacks anymore! Read on and find out how. . . .

D0011788

ANXIETY & PANIC ATTACKS

THEIR CAUSE AND CURE

The Five-Point Life-Plus Program
for Conquering Fear

ROBERT HANDLY
with Pauline Neff

FAWCETT

BALLANTINE BOOKS • NEW YORK

A Fawcett Book
Published by The Random House Publishing Group
Copyright © 1985 by Robert Handly and Pauline Neff

Published in the United States by Fawcett Books, an imprint of The Random House Publishing Group, a division of Random House, Inc., New York, and simultaneously in Canada by Random House of Canada Limited, Toronto.

FAWCETT is a registered trademark and the Fawcett colophon is a trademark of Random House, Inc.

ISBN 978-0-449-21331-5

This edition published by arrangement with Rawson Associates, a division of the Scribner Book Companies, Inc.

Printed in the United States of America

www.ballantinebooks.com

First Ballantine Books Edition: June 1987

OPM 39 38 37 36 35 34

For Dad,
whose loving memory I cherish

The greatest revolution of our generation is the discovery that human beings, by changing the inner attitudes of their minds, can change the outer aspects of their lives.

WILLIAM JAMES

CONTENTS

~~~~~~

ACKNOWLEDGMENTS

This book is a direct result of my personal transformation, and I want to thank those people who played a part in it. First and foremost, I thank my wife, Cindy, for her unwavering faith, love, and strength that have sustained me. I also thank Jim Wilson, who showed me a better way; Mother, for her prayers and unconditional love; and Neva Davis, for teaching and sharing. I'm especially grateful to Maxwell Maltz and Napoleon Hill, whose books gave me inspiration.

My dream to share my story could not have happened without the special talent, patience, and care of my coauthor, Pauline Neff. My gratitude to her is felt at the deepest level I am capable of feeling. I also wish especially to thank Johnnie Godwin for his professional guidance and editorial comments in getting me on the right track. Thanks also to Toni Sciarra and Eleanor Rawson for their tremendous help and editorial suggestions.

PART I

The Five-Point Program for Conquering Fear

CHAPTER 1

~~~~~~

The High Price
of Panic

A well-dressed executive fidgets at the boardroom table. A heated discussion is in progress, but for some reason he can't seem to understand what the other directors are saying.

"What's the matter with me? I can't concentrate! If I keep on like this, my presentation is going to be lousy. My stomach feels like one big knot!" he groans to himself.

A college student shuffles frantically through the examination papers she has just received.

"It looks like Greek! I studied. I really did. But now I can't answer a single question. I think I'm going to faint. My heart's racing out of control."

A young mother stands in the line at the supermarket.

"Six people ahead of me and the baby won't stop crying. I can't stand this waiting. Everyone's staring at me. I feel as though I'm going to pass out."

These reactions are the symptoms of panic. You have it, but you don't know why. You may have it in a mild form that is little more than anxiety—sweaty palms, a queasy stomach, lightheadedness that prevents you from thinking clearly, a rapidly beating heart that causes you to toss in bed.

Or you may experience panic in terrifying attacks. Suddenly you feel as if you will faint. Your heart pounds so hard you fear cardiac arrest. Your breathing turns into hyperventilating. Your mind goes haywire with the awful thought that you are about to lose control—perhaps tear off your clothing, drive your car off the road, or shout obscenities in public.

The first time you have a panic attack you may go to the doctor, only to be told there's nothing physically wrong. So you try to reason with yourself: "If nothing is wrong with me, then I'll just try to stay calm and the panic attacks will go away." But it seems the harder you try, the more frequently they return.

Next, you may try the "Well, that's just the way life is" rationale. "There are just too many people crowding our overpopulated earth. We live in a hurry-up, live-it-up, do-or-die society that doesn't care about anything anymore. No wonder I'm anxious," you say.

But this explanation doesn't change the way you feel. Your anxiety continues. Soon everything hurts, from your stomach to your head to your back. Your blood pressure goes up and your mood goes down. You can't sleep. You feel worse and worse.

Eventually you just try to cope. There's always a tranquilizer, a painkiller, another pack of cigarettes, a stiff drink or two, or even a snort of cocaine to help you cope with panic. Or you can scream at your kids or spouse, eat everything in sight, or sleep twelve hours a day to try to escape from all the bad feelings.

Or you may develop phobias, unreasonable fears of flying or riding in elevators or crossing bridges. Your queasy stomach may evolve into colitis or ulcers. Your high blood pressure may bring on a heart attack. Your tension headache may become a migraine, and your back tension may become a permanent spasm condition.

You might even develop the most serious panic disorder, *a fear of fear itself*—at its most severe a phobia that keeps you imprisoned in your home, afraid that if you go outside you will have another panic attack.

But you cope. You go to the doctor and get a prescription. Why try to fight? That's just the way life is.

The Strange Facts about Panic Disorders

The dictionary definition of panic is "a sudden overpowering fright, especially a sudden terror often inspired by a trifling cause or a misapprehension of danger and accompanied by unreasoning or frantic efforts to secure safety."

Surprisingly, the millions who experience panic disorders might agree that the causes of their sudden overpowering symptoms of anxiety can be "trifling." They know that they should *not* sense danger from such low-level annoyances as disagreeing with their spouse, standing in line at the supermarket, or giving a public speech. Their bodies should *not* react with symptoms that prevent them from functioning normally. Yet anxiety and panic disorders are a fact of life. The most recent National Institute of Mental Health report indicates that one in nine adults harbors some kind of phobia, making it the *most common mental health problem* in the United States, even ahead of alcoholism. And many professionals believe that a large percentage of alcoholics are "closet" phobics who mask their problems with drink or abuse of other substances.

Phobias and other panic disorders *do* keep people from living normally. They *do* interfere with personal relationships and open the door to more serious illnesses. I have never met anyone who suffered from an anxiety or panic disorder who did not want to get rid of it. The problem is that most people don't know how.

My Method for Dealing with Anxiety

The method for preventing anxiety or recovering from panic disorders which I describe in this book is based primarily on behavioral psychology, but it also includes the principles of positive thinking, cognitive restructuring (or rational thinking, in layman's terms), and the creative use of the unconscious mind. Some of these techniques are taught at the Phobia Center of the Southwest, in Dallas, with which I have been associated. This group of psychotherapists and other professionals has helped more than thirteen hundred people overcome all kinds of phobias. Because I have completely recovered from agoraphobia, the most serious kind of panic disorder, I serve as living proof that a return not only to a normal life but to a *better* life is possible. I want to show you how you can recover, too.

I will also describe certain exercises that were of special help to me. I have consolidated all of these methods into what I call my Five-Point Program, which in turn is based on Five Basic Principles. In subsequent chapters I will explain how to use these principles. You should be able to gain some insight into the situations in your life that are triggering your anxiety by studying these principles and answering the questions and checklists I will provide. Although you may not be able to alter the situations, you can use the Five Basic Principles to change your *reactions* to them. Whether you are experiencing simple anxiety or a complex panic disorder, you can use these aids to regain control over your life.

My Experience with Panic

My panic attacks began, as they do for most people, without warning. I was thirty-three years old. To an outsider, I must have appeared to have no problems at all. In fact, my life seemed more successful than most. Six years before, I had left the executive search firm for which I worked and set myself up in my own business. Right away I made placements. I had a loving, supportive wife named Cindy and a beautiful home. We golfed, traveled, and enjoyed plenty of friends. People thought of me as a fun-loving guy who had everything going for him. Good old Bob. What a success!

Inside, I felt just the opposite. To me it seemed as if everyone else could do almost anything better than I could. I lived with self-doubt, insecurity, and feelings of inferiority. I saw myself as not being as "together" as a lot of other people, not as capable. When good things happened to me, I told myself I didn't deserve them. Everything depended on luck.

I didn't realize it at the time, but now I know that a lot of my feelings of inferiority came from my childhood experiences. I was born clubfooted. Although surgery eventually corrected my foot, I was left with a slightly withered leg. As a child I took a lot of abuse because of that leg. I came to feel inferior and insecure. Somehow I developed a habit of believing that I couldn't do the things I wanted to do. After college I had six different jobs in seven years. I looked good when I went to interview for the position of salesman, even sales manager. I started out great. But within a year, I just wasn't producing.

If other people saw me as successful now that I had my own business, I knew I was a fraud. The reason I worked for myself, I was convinced, was because I couldn't work for anyone else. And I wasn't making nearly as much money as I thought I should. I continually berated myself for what I saw as my failures. Anxiety, depression, and feelings of inferiority were my constant companions.

As for my physical condition, I thought that colitis, or something just as bad, was a condition everyone had. My stomach churned every day, but it was no big deal; the coating medication I swallowed soothed the savage beast.

My First Attack

The day I suffered my first attack of agoraphobia, I was in my usual frame of mind. As I dodged expressway traffic on the way to the office, I mentally cursed every car that cut in front of me. When one almost sideswiped me, I really let him have it.

"You idiot!" I yelled, shaking my fist at him. Then I told myself, "If you don't watch out for those guys, you'll end up in a hospital, and then what will you do about those two placements?"

For the past four months I had been nursing along two executives who were going to earn me a big fee of $30,000 to $40,000 once they went to work for the two companies that had openings. I should have been congratulating myself that I had two good prospects. Instead, I warned myself of all the things that could go wrong to make the deals fall through and leave me empty-handed. If anyone had told me I was being negative by worrying that way, I would have denied it. I was simply trying to spot problems before they happened, so that I could plan for them.

I was definitely going to have to do something about Dick, the most promising prospect. Lately he had been hinting that he might be able to negotiate a raise from the company he now worked for rather than take the position I was selling him. If only I could persuade the hiring company to offer him more, Dick wouldn't have to think twice. I had to do just that today, I thought, feeling my hands tighten on the steering wheel.

And take Jim, the other prospect. It looked as if the company I hoped to place him with was going to fill the position from within its own ranks. Damn it! Somehow I needed to make them see how valuable an employee he would be for them. I had too much time invested in both these deals to lose them now.

As I walked into my office building, I didn't even notice the Christmas tree set up in the foyer. December wasn't anything to get excited about anyway. The holidays were bound to depress my mother even more. She had been almost suicidal ever since my father's death from a heart attack a year ago. I had persuaded Mother to move to Dallas so that Cindy and I could help her recover. But nothing I did seemed to help very much. I felt guilty because she was depressed.

Furthermore, I missed Dad, too. He had been a wonderful father. Even though I rarely went to him for advice, just knowing that he was there had been my support. He had been my Rock of Gibraltar. Now he was gone, and I had the further responsibility of helping Mother. No matter what I said, I couldn't seem to lift her despondency. Even worse, I often felt myself becoming impatient with her. Why was I so unreasonable?

In my office I opened my briefcase, got out some papers, and stared at the wall. Too bad that the employees who used to work for me were gone. After I hired them, I discovered that they had so many personal problems I had to waste hours listening to their troubles. Finally I encouraged them to find other jobs. Still, it was lonely being the only person in the office.

Nonchalantly I put my feet on my desk and began to read the *Wall Street Journal.* And then it happened. With no warning, my heart began to pound. Perspiration broke out on my forehead. My stomach flopped over. I bolted upright while my mind raced out of control with fantasies of childhood's worst demon—ending with a vision of my father's pale face in his coffin. *What was happening to me?*

Dimly, as in a dream, I heard the phone ringing. I picked it up and heard my mother's voice. It sounded far away. "My God, Mother, something awful is happening to me. I feel as if I'm going to black out!" I gasped. Mother's voice leaped two octaves.

"Oh, Bob, is it your heart?" My heart. Yes, Mother had had a heart attack. Dad had died of a heart attack at fifty-eight. Now it was my turn!

"Oh, yes, that's it. It must be my heart!"

"I'm coming," Mother screamed. The few minutes before she arrived seemed like hours. My heart was pounding out of my chest. Perspiration streamed down my face. I wanted to jump up and run out of the office, but at the same time I was afraid I would faint.

The Wrong Diagnosis

Oddly enough, by the time Mother came, my heart had calmed. I was able to walk shakily to her car. At the doctor's office, I felt as good as ever. None of the electrocardiograms, blood pressure readings, or probings showed anything wrong with me at all!

"You've probably been working too hard," the doctor told me.

"Yeah, maybe so," I said, feeling relieved but embarrassed. Mother drove me back to the office and dropped me off. But the minute I got inside the elevator, my heart began to crash against my chest again. Fear gripped me. The stupid doctor was wrong! I was going to die, right here on this elevator! I jabbed the button for the next floor. I staggered out into the hall and burst into the closest office, clutching at my heart.

"Call my wife, I'm going to pass out!" I shouted at the startled receptionist. While she dialed the number I gave her, I collapsed, gasping, on the sofa. My mouth was so dry I couldn't swallow. I waited for the blackness to hit me, wondering if I would ever regain consciousness. Instead, my heart began to slow. By the time Cindy arrived, I felt almost myself. She drove me home, making sympathetic noises. Back at the house I felt fantastically good. We both were confused by what had happened.

That night was like any other. The next morning I told myself I was going to be okay. I would go to the office. I would be in control of myself. But this time I only reached the door of the office building when the strange symptoms returned. And with them came a terrible, unreasoning fear. It was as if someone were holding a loaded gun to my head and I was watching him squeeze the trigger. Yet what was there to fear? I drove immediately to the doctor.

"You've got to do something," I told him.

"Bob, I can't find anything physically wrong with you," he insisted. "It must be nerves. Here, try these tranquilizers."

I took as many tranquilizers as I dared, but every time I went to the office, the strange "heart attacks" began again. Now they happened elsewhere, too. Cindy and I went out to eat, but by the time we waited in line and got a table, I was so uncomfortable we had to leave. We tried to do some Christmas shopping one evening, but my heart raced so fast I ran out of the shopping mall into the night. In the movies, I felt I had to grip the arms of my seat to keep from jumping up and shouting obscenities when the panicky feeling hit me. Maybe the doctor was right. I was nervous . . . maybe even *crazy!*

The Avoidance Syndrome

Now Cindy and I could no longer play cards with friends or visit relatives because the terrible panic always returned. I tried to force myself to go to my office, numb with tranquilizers, but I couldn't function there. After six months, I gave up. I stayed at home in my "safe place."

While I hid in the house, my business plummeted. I needed to be making calls on companies and interviewing executives, but even walking into the front yard for the newspapers was fraught with terror for me.

Throughout all this turmoil, Cindy was truly sympathetic. She didn't pressure me. She didn't say, "Of course you can go to work. Just go ahead and try it." Now that I know more about phobias, I realize she did the right thing. But we were both so afraid of what was going to happen that we simply stopped talking about my problem. Cindy had a good job as an administrative manager with a federal law office and we had savings to live on, but my feeling of self-worth hit zero. Every morning when she left, her look of pity made me feel like a complete failure.

Now depression set in. Every morning I awoke to fear. I despaired. I couldn't eat. Life itself tasted bad. Suicide seemed my only escape.

My Key to Recovery

Then one morning I opened the newspaper and saw an article about a strange illness called agoraphobia. The story described a woman whose symptoms were just like mine. Every time she tried to go to the grocery store or drive in a car pool, she felt her heart pound. She almost fainted. She broke out in a sweat. She felt as if she were going out of control. To avoid these misery-producing attacks, she began to stay at home. Eventually she was housebound, just as I was.

But the article also said she had found a way to stop the attacks. Jim Wilson, a psychotherapist with the Phobia Center of the Southwest, in Dallas, had showed her that the illness was simply the body's response to overwhelming stress. He didn't remove her stress, but he taught her techniques to cope with it. Now she could dine in restaurants, drive her children home from school, even participate in the PTA. She was living just like a normal person! I was so excited that I raced to the phone to make an immediate appointment with Jim Wilson.

I liked Jim on sight. A tall, calm, but vibrant man, he did not seem at all surprised when I told him my symptoms. After a few simple questions he assured me that I wasn't crazy. I actually did suffer from agoraphobia. My illness had a name and it had a cure!

As Jim described what I needed to do, I saw that the problem I had thought was physical was actually caused both by the body and the mind. First, Jim explained that a panic attack was a *normal* reaction of the *body* to danger. Second, he told me I needed to learn to depend on the deepest level of my own *mind*—not my will and determination—to control the circumstances in my life that were in fact controlling me. And third, I needed to use both my *mind* and *body* to desensitize myself to my fear of leaving my "safe place."

The Cure That Led to Life Plus

During the six months in which I had been unable to work, I paid a high price for having panic attacks. I had been so depressed I had even contemplated suicide. Now that I look back, however, I realize that the high price I was paying was also the first step toward self-discovery that was going to lead not only to my recovery, but to a completely new way of life that was so wonderful I could only call it "Life Plus."

I'll have more to say about the possibility that you can achieve Life Plus in later chapters. Right now, just let me tell you what happened to me after Life Plus dawned on me in 1979. I was so excited about my complete recovery that I began to tell others what had happened to me. When clients or friends told me they were worried . . . or their stomachs were tied in knots . . . or they had a spastic colon . . . or chronic diarrhea . . . or migraines and depression . . . or a hectic family life, I shared the struggles I had gone through with my panic disorder. Then they opened up to me and told me the fears in their own lives. Often they hadn't admitted to having these problems even to their own spouses or best friends.

For the first time in their lives, these friends were now able to relax and enjoy their children, their spouses, their in-laws, their careers, their hobbies, their health. Then I saw that I was able to reach out and help others. I was living like the confident people I used to envy. I was enjoying life myself.

I then joined with Jim Wilson and his partner, Dr. Robert Ingram, in the Phobia Center of the Southwest. We began to hold seminars for corporations that wanted to teach their employees how to deal with stress and anxiety. I, who had always been terrified of public speaking, began to tell my experiences before groups of agoraphobics. I plunged headlong into a new career as a human resources educator, and I loved it. Gradually I refined the knowledge I had gained from Jim Wilson and my experiences in using the creative powers of the mind to overcome panic into what I call my Five-Point Program. In this way, others could easily grasp the methods I used to overcome panic and find Life Plus.

If you have a burning desire to get over your panic attacks, my Five-Point Program will almost certainly help you. You will no longer have to say, "That's just the way life is," and suffer the discomfort of anxiety or the agony of panic attacks. You will be in a position to gain Life Plus as I did.

CHAPTER 2

~~~~~~

"What's Wrong with Me?"

Your anxiety may be just as excruciating as mine was, or it may be much less so. After reading about what happened to me, you may even be wondering whether or not your symptoms indicate that you have a panic disorder. By reading the anxiety checklist below and marking the statements true or false on a piece of paper, you can see just where you are on the anxiety roller coaster:

1. I often feel tired even though I have had a good night's sleep.
2. Sometimes my heart seems to race out of control even though my doctor says I don't have a heart problem.
3. I often have insomnia.
4. I have bouts of backache that hit me for no apparent reason.

5. Indigestion, diarrhea, or headache frequently keep me from functioning at my best.
6. I can face some situations in my life without hyperventilating or "going all to pieces" only with the help of a tranquilizer or a good, stiff drink.
7. I have one or more relationships that cause me to feel nervous at times.
8. I frequently work later than my coworkers and often bring work home.
9. I have at least one bad habit that I have not been able to break.
10. Secretly, I just don't believe I measure up to other people I see.

Did you mark most of those statements as true about yourself? If so, you could be suffering from the beginning stages of a panic disorder. The first step toward achieving freedom from it is to recognize that you *need* to change. The second is to realize that you can *choose* to change. And the third is to *make a commitment* to change. Come on! Soar with the eagles! Go after all the riches, love, happiness, peace, success, good health, and self-esteem that you deserve. All it takes from you at this point is a decision that you are going to change.

Questions You May Be Asking

Now that I am in the profession of helping others recover from panic attacks, I realize that the questions I so desperately wanted Jim Wilson to answer for me are the same ones asked by everyone else I meet who has this crippling disorder.

On my first visit to Jim's office, my mind was literally running over with demands for the information that I had long ago stopped requesting from doctors. The ones I consulted did not have any answers for me.

I didn't discuss my condition with friends or family either. When I talked with others I could not convince them that I really was suffering as if I were having a heart attack or that I was going to faint or stop breathing. Too many well-meaning friends told me, "Look, Bob, the doctor says nothing is wrong. Get up. Get control. You can get over this thing." When I told them I had tried and still had these symptoms, I could see them shaking their heads over me. I imagined they were saying to themselves, "Poor old Bob. He's really cracked up."

This may have happened to you, too. That's why I'll answer the questions that may be ready to erupt in your mind before I tell you what Jim told me about panic disorders.

If I have panic attacks, does that mean I am going crazy?

No. It means you may have a chemical imbalance that predisposes you to feeling anxious. It also means you are not coping with stress in a constructive way so as to prevent your anxiety from becoming panic. You are not mentally ill, but if the fear that you have is irrational and keeps you from doing normal everyday things that most people take for granted, you may have a phobia. Phobias are considered psychiatric disorders and can cover a multitude of situations. But the good news is that behavioral psychologists consider phobias the most treatable of all the psychiatric disorders. These psychologists do not brand you with a diagnosis of anxiety neurosis or depression—conditions that could require extensive psychoanalysis. Instead, they teach you mental tools to overcome your physical symptoms.

But what are the physical causes of panic?

Because no research has definitely proven the etiology of panic attacks, the theories about their physical cause range from hormonal and chemical imbalances to disabilities such as mitral valve prolapse, hypoglycemia, hyperthyroidism, anemia, or hypersensitivity to caffeine.

There is good evidence to show that the vulnerability or susceptibility to panic attacks is what is called a physiologic sensitivity abnormality. In recent studies it has been shown that panic symptoms can be induced in people who have experienced panic attacks by introducing certain substances into their systems, such as sodium lactate or CO_2. There is also evidence to indicate that this physical sensitivity is inherited. Studies show that people who have relatives who have panic attacks have a one in four risk of developing a panic disorder, whereas the general population has only a 2 percent incidence.

Because 70 percent of those who have phobias are women, whose panic episodes are more frequent just before the menstrual period and during early childbearing years when progesterone levels are high, some physicians link this female hormone to panic disorder. Other doctors, noting that the level of adrenaline is abnormally high at all times in the blood of both male and female agoraphobics, believe these patients have a brain dysfunction. It is as if they have a faulty thermostat that fails to shut off the production of adrenaline at the proper time, leaving the patient subject to panic attacks.

Many professionals are the first to admit that they have a problem in determining whether patients have a panic disorder or a physical problem such as mitral valve prolapse or hypoglycemia, which can cause panic symptoms to occur. The symptoms of hypoglycemia—nervousness, anxiety of panic proportions, shakiness, palpitations, sweating, weakness, and unsteadiness—are much the same.

Similarly, symptoms of mitral valve prolapse, a bulging of a cardiac valve (which current research indicates is usually a benign condition), include dizziness, palpitations, shortness of breath, fatigue, and panic. At the 1984 meeting of the Phobia Society of America, Dr. Frederic Neuman, associate director of the White Plains Phobia Clinic, reported a high incidence of mitral valve prolapse and hypoglycemia in the general population. He concluded that undoubtedly many people have these physical conditions and also a panic disorder at the same time. They may need to be treated for *both* problems. If you have a physical condition that causes you to feel panicky, plus a chemical predisposition, you could develop a panic disorder unless you learn some coping skills.

Behavioral psychologists, on the other hand, believe that if you have a panic disorder, you simply have a learned response to an irrational fear. In other words, they look at an anxiety attack as a habit—you are so accustomed to experiencing the anxiety caused by your chemical imbalance that you don't try to fight it. You don't even know that by coping with stress differently, you can avoid these feelings. You get into an anxiety spiral that eventually results in a true panic disorder. Behavioral psychologists teach you to condition yourself to respond to fear in a different way, just as you can condition yourself to stop biting your fingernails.

Just as you may inherit a chemical imbalance, you may be born more sensitive than others. Or you may inherit or be reared to acquire the personality of a perfectionist or people-pleaser, always trying to make others happy. These traits load you in favor of having a panic disorder. But you can learn new ways of thinking to help you overcome it.

Since I overcame my agoraphobia by coupling the techniques of behavioral psychologists with some of my own, I believe that panic attacks are *mental dysfunctions with physical symptoms.* When you worry, think negatively, or have improper attitudes toward stress, you produce vivid mental pictures of the situation you fear. Your body becomes aroused just as if the situation you imagine is actually happening. Then it releases adrenaline, which brings on the *physical* anxiety symptoms. Therefore, if you can eliminate worry, negative thinking, and improper attitudes toward stress with your mind, you can overcome much of the anxiety that brings on a panic attack.

Just what exactly is the process by which your mind causes your body to create physical problems?

If you have a lot of stress and do not know how to cope with it, your body becomes aroused because it is being bombarded with anxiety-producing stimuli. Nature's purpose in allowing the body to become aroused is protection. When faced with sudden danger, you become physically ready to react by either fighting the stressor or fleeing from it. When the brain puts into action what is called the "fight or flight" response, it releases hormones known as corticosteroids. These powerful hormones constrict the blood vessels in the peripheral parts of the body in order to drive blood into the brain and deep down into the large muscles for added strength. The heart pounds, digestion shuts down, breathing increases, and muscles tighten.

The fight or flight response progresses in three stages. The first stage is the *alarm stage* as described above. If the emergency is suddenly resolved, and you escape from the danger, your body reverses the alarm stage and sends the physical conditions back to normal. If the threat persists, however, a second stage, known as the *resistance stage*, appears. The physiological responses such as muscle tension and digestive conditions become fixed. If the body is forced to maintain a stage of resistance for too long a period or if the threat is repeated often enough, a final *ex-*

haustion stage develops. The body can no longer adapt to the threat, and the systems collapse.

Because of hereditary predisposition and environmental factors, everyone's system reacts differently to the exhaustion caused by poorly managed stress. Some people are "muscle reactors," some "gut reactors," and some "vascular reactors." And some have panic attacks.

Muscle reactors constantly brace their skeletal muscles, such as in the neck and shoulders, causing tension headaches. In some cases, the tension moves down the spine. (Amazingly, this is the cause of up to 95 percent of all low back pain!) Not knowing how to relax, these people become constantly frustrated in their attempts to relieve their hurting muscles. Thus they build up more frustration, causing more bracing and more pain.

Gut reactors, of course, are those who constantly brace the muscles of the stomach and intestine and suffer ulcers or colitis.

The vascular reactors are those who constantly brace the smooth muscles such as the arteries in response to stress. They suffer the excruciating pain of a migraine headache when the inner blood vessels in their brain constrict, pushing blood into the outer cranial vessels, which in turn are forced to dilate beyond their normal capacity. Vascular reactors may also have chronically cold hands and feet.

Many scientists also believe that chronic bodily arousal depresses the immune system, which they maintain makes the body vulnerable to cancer, high blood pressure, high cholesterol, heart attacks, and strokes. Even if you are not suffering severe anxiety or panic attacks, it makes sense to learn mental techniques for reducing the physical effects of stress.

But since a biochemical imbalance is involved, couldn't medications be used to prevent panic attacks and other stress-related symptoms?

Yes, doctors have discovered medications that do prevent panic attacks. In the early 1970s, Dr. Donald Klein of the Columbia Medical Center in New York discovered that panic attacks could be prevented by using Imipramine (Tofranil), a tricyclic antidepressant. Later the monoamine oxidase (MAO) inhibitor types of antidepressant (marketed under the names Nardil and Parnate) were found to be even more potent in blocking panic attacks.

These discoveries have not, however, revolutionized the treatment of panic disorders. The problem is that antidepressants of both types have multiple side effects, including increased heart rate, dizziness, shakiness, blurred vision, dry mouth, and headaches. Since patients experience many of these same symptoms when they have a panic attack, many are unwilling to take these medications either at all or in sufficient quantities.

Although doctors do prescribe traditional Benzodiazepine tranquilizers (Valium, Librium, Serax, Ativan, and the like) for panic attacks, these have not been found, either clinically or experimentally, to block panic attacks. But they do diminish the anticipatory anxiety—the stress caused by anticipating or fearing the panic symptoms—and patients do not object to taking them. But patients who depend on tranquilizers seldom get well, because the medication does not block panic attacks. Frequently they depend on tranquilizers for years to help them avoid dealing with their illness and disability. All the while their condition may deteriorate.

The medical treatment of panic disorders and agoraphobia improved dramatically in the early 1980s with the introduction of a new medication, Alprazolam (Xanax), that is in a class by itself. Structurally it resembles the Benzodiazepine tranquilizers, but clinically it acts like the anti-depressants. It does block panic. Two studies showed that Xanax also improved depressed mood as effectively as Tofranil and Elavil.

The side effects of Xanax are similar to those of tranquilizers. It causes sedation, which can be controlled by reducing the dose. Doctors start with a very low dose (half of a .25 mg tablet), taken in divided doses four times a day after a meal or snack. They gradually increase to a fully effective dose of 4 to 8 mg per day, depending on the individual's need and ability to tolerate it. Like all tranquilizers, Xanax is physiologically addictive. When the patient is taken off Xanax, he or she must taper off slowly to avoid withdrawal symptoms. Doctors who advocate the use of Xanax feel this side effect is a small price to pay when compared to the potential for alleviation of all panic symptoms in the majority of patients.

One study has found that reduced dosages of Xanax could be used in conjunction with drugs called beta blockers, such as Inderal. But more research is needed to see if the two drugs used together will truly block panic attacks while reducing side effects. Since researchers have not yet identified the physical abnormal sensitivity that causes panic attacks, the condition cannot be "cured" with the medications now being prescribed. Most patients who take medication for panic attacks have as their long-range goal to be free of symptoms without using drugs. But even a patient who has been symptom-free for years may suffer an unexpected relapse and experience a brief panic attack. For this reason, even doctors who believe strongly in treatment with medication often advise their patients to learn behavioral therapy techniques to prevent anxiety and panic.

If a patient has gone off medication and then experiences another attack, these doctors will advise going back on the medication for a while. Or they may tell patients to carry medication with them to use only in emergencies. They feel that even though some people have been successfully treated without medication, for most individuals drugs expedite the behavioral education that is part of treatment. They believe that medication is absolutely necessary for patients whose symptoms are severe.

Many professionals feel strongly pro or con about prescribing medications for panic attacks. At the 1984 meeting of the Phobia Society of America, the opposing sides would agree only to keep an open mind about treatment methods.

What kind of professional help do you advocate?

By all means go to a good internist to discover whether you have a physical condition that causes panic symptoms. Let me warn you, however, that some professionals do not understand phobias or anxiety symptoms. You could wind up with a bunch of tranquilizers, as I did. They make you numb without ever overcoming your feeling that you are on the verge of exploding with anxiety. Other anxious people spend several years in analysis seeking to find the "missing link" between a traumatic childhood event and their present emotional problems. I'm not knocking psychiatry or psychology. In fact, I went to a psychologist myself to learn some techniques for dealing with my phobia. And when I used these behavioral tools, I recovered fairly quickly. I'm simply urging you to be aware of what you may encounter when you seek help.

If you describe symptoms of a panic attack to some doctors, the only alternative they see is to prescribe drugs. I do not believe this is always the best solution. After one session with Jim to learn why I was having panic attacks and what I could do about them, I never had to go back. If you have a true panic disorder, in my opinion you may have a biochemical imbalance, but you would still not have a panic disorder unless you had developed the habit of coping poorly with stress. You can overcome habits! You aren't crazy, and you don't necessarily need long sessions with a professional.

Since I fully recovered from a severe case of agoraphobia without medication, I advocate what I call a holistic approach to recovery. I believe in aiming for both physical fitness and mental reconditioning to achieve a cure. Although I recognize that people who have suffered from panic attacks for a long time might benefit by taking drugs to prevent the attacks while they are learning mental reconditioning, I wonder if the risks are worth it. Will you really try to change the long-ingrained behavior patterns that exacerbate your panic attacks if the medication blocks them? Isn't the temptation to put up with the side effects of the medication and live a kind of half-life instead of being able to enjoy all the wonders of living? In my opinion, you should use drugs to block panic attacks only if you promise yourself you will give them up entirely as quickly as possible. By joining a support group, you will be more likely to reach this goal. For more information on support groups, look in Chapter 8 under "Tips for Acting As If."

What is the difference between panic symptoms and a phobia?

It's a matter of degree. Both conditions are a reaction to an irrational fear, and both may result in your feeling highly nervous, disoriented, or so terrified that you temporarily cannot function as a normal person. You progress from panic symptoms to a phobia only when you start *avoiding* the idea, situation, or external object on which your irrational fear is focused.

Sometimes it is hard to recognize whether you really have a phobia. Pauline Neff never realized that she had a phobia about public speaking until she started helping me write this book. She knew that whenever she stood before a live audience, her voice shook, her hands perspired, and her knees trembled so badly she almost collapsed. The result was that she avoided making speeches. Then she joined a Toastmasters International club and with the help of supportive members desensitized herself to her fear. Pauline got over her phobia without ever realizing she had one!

A very competent executive whom I could never place with another company would have been surprised to know that he had a phobia, too. He simply fell apart on interviews. His heart raced, he felt disoriented, he stammered, and he couldn't make rational answers to questions. At the time I knew him, I didn't how what a phobia was either. I didn't realize how simple it would have been for him to get over his phobia about interviews and find a position for which he was fully qualified.

I also know a beautiful young woman with a fantastic figure and personality who never had a date. Even the prospect of going out made her so nervous she started hyperventilating. Until she got help, she didn't know she had a phobia either.

You may have symptoms of anxiety without having a phobia. You just feel a bit lightheaded when you have to wait in a line. You have a slight feeling you are going to black out when you go to a party and you don't know anyone there. Your heart races when you lie in bed at night worrying over your business, your personal relationships, or your future. I felt this way many times before I had a genuine panic attack. But I didn't have a true phobia until I began to avoid going places where I experienced the attacks. You don't have a phobia either until you start avoiding whatever it is you fear.

Many people who have a simple phobia are successful at avoiding the one situation—the public speaking, the interview, the date, the eating alone, the riding an elevator, or the flying in an airplane—that brings on their anxiety. They function at a level they call normal even if they are not achieving their true potential.

But if you are avoiding one such situation, you may be in real trouble when some crisis requires you to face it. For instance, you may have been telling yourself you can't stand up in front of people and talk coherently. What happens when your boss requires you to make a speech? Or let's say you believe you "can't" go in for an interview. What would happen if you lost the job you have now? Or, if a young woman panics at the idea of being alone with men, what will she do if she has to work in a place where many of her fellow employees and business contacts are men?

In such a situation, you could force yourself to make a speech, go for an interview, or associate with men. But if you keep telling yourself how nervous you feel about it, you may be setting yourself up for a real panic disorder. Your negative thinking will only encourage your unconscious to produce more anxiety. In Chapter 4, I will explain in greater detail how your unconscious can cause you to have anxiety even when you tell yourself you won't. Right now the important thing to recognize is that if you have a situation that you're avoiding because it brings on anxiety, you can do something about it before it gets worse.

Okay, so I have some anxiety. But isn't it really rather rare for such symptoms to develop into a disabling phobia?

You'd be surprised. About 28 million Americans suffer from phobias, which have been called the disease of the decade. "What schizophrenia was to the 1960's, what depression and burnout were to the 1970's, phobias are to the 1980's," said *Newsweek* in its April 23, 1984, issue.

Of the several different classifications of phobias, *agoraphobia*, which I had, is first in terms of the number of people who have it. Fully 70 percent of all phobics have agoraphobia.

Contrary to the definitions you might find in a dictionary, agoraphobia is not a fear of the marketplace or of open places. Agoraphobia is simply the fear of fear. Agoraphobics are so afraid that they will have another panic attack that they avoid going to the place where they had the first one. As they continue to have anxiety symptoms, they gradually eliminate more and more places, until at last they are confined to their "safe place," usually their home.

The second most common classification is *simple phobias*, which involve fear and avoidance limited to one or two situations. You may experience such terrifying panic when you ride an elevator that you start walking up ten flights of stairs instead. You may so fear flying in a plane that you waste precious hours riding buses and trains across the continent. Bridges may seem so scary that you have to turn the wheel of your car over to someone else whenever you approach one.

Animal phobias, the next most prevalent classification, are a fear of bugs, snakes, dogs, and other creatures. Usually these phobias begin in childhood and simply continue into adulthood. *Social phobias* are the fear of such situations as public speaking or eating alone in a restaurant.

Whether you have any one of these phobias or slight anxiety symptoms, you can benefit by learning the same techniques I learned to get over my agoraphobia.

I have a lot of stress in my life. Could that be responsible for my panic attacks?

Many people who suffer panic attacks blame stress for their problems, but blaming stress does not present the whole picture. The late Hans Selye, M.D., the leading researcher on stress, found that stress was an inevitable part of every person's life. No one can escape it. In fact, Selye called stress "the spice of life," the great motivator that may cause us to achieve great things.

Scientists distinguish between *eustress*, which does not cause panic attacks, and *distress*, which does. If you have eustress, you may experience anxiety from life events, but because of your attitude toward the stressors, you can deal with them and let go of them. If you suffer from distress, however, you constantly brace yourself against the life events that cause you discomfort. Your perception of the stressor as an extreme danger which you must either flee or fight causes your sympathetic nervous system to release hormones, such as adrenaline and noradrenaline, which prepare you for action. These hormones signal your body to send all its oxygen supply to your muscles and your liver to release extra sugar, the emergency fuel for the muscles. Your heart rate increases dramatically and your blood pressure shoots up. Blood levels of uric acid are increased, and histamine is produced. Your blood is suddenly capable of clotting faster, too.

Such constant bracing against stressful life events makes you subject to panic attacks. I am convinced that after my father died, I felt overwhelmed with stress and I braced against it. Not knowing how to deal with stress brought on my first panic attack.

If you have an abnormal number of stressful events in your life and don't know how to cope with them, you are at greater risk of having a panic attack. Look over the *Social Readjustment Rating Scale* below and see how much stress the life events you have experienced during the past year have caused you. Please note that when the word "change" is used in this list, it means *both* positive and negative changes. Even positive changes cause stress.

If you score below 150 points on this scale, you have about a one in three chance of serious health change (including panic attacks) in the next two years. If you score

Social Readjustment Rating Scale

Life Event	Mean Value
Death of spouse	100
Divorce	73
Marital separation	65
Jail term	63
Death of close family member	63
Personal injury or illness	53
Marriage	50
Fired at work	47
Marital reconciliations	45
Retirement	45
Change in health of family member	44
Pregnancy	40
Sex difficulties	39
Gain of new family member	39
Business readjustment	39
Change in financial state	38
Death of close friend	37
Change to different line of work	36
Change in number of arguments with spouse	35
Mortgage or loan for major purchase (home, etc.)	31
Foreclosure of mortgage or loan	30
Change in responsibilities at work	29
Son or daughter leaving home	29
Trouble with in-laws	29
Outstanding personal achievement	28
Wife begins or stops work	26
Begin or end school	26
Change in living conditions	25
Revision of personal habits	24
Trouble with boss	23
Change in work hours or conditions	20
Change in residence	20
Change in schools	20
Change in recreation	19
Change in church activities	19
Change in social activities	18
Mortgage or loan for lesser purchase (car, TV, etc.)	17

Life Event	Mean Value
Change in sleeping habits	16
Change in number of family get-togethers	15
Change in eating habits	15
Vacation	13
Christmas	12
Minor violations of the law	11

(Reprinted by permission from T. H. Holmes and R. H. Rahe, "The Social Readjustment Rating Scale," *Journal of Psychosomatic Research*, Vol. 11:213–218 [1967], Pergamon Press, Inc., as revised)

between 150 and 300 points, your chances increase to 50/50. If you score over 300 points, your chances are an overwhelming 90 percent—*unless* you learn some coping skills.

If you rated high on this scale, do not despair. Remember, your *attitude* toward these life events determines whether you have *distress* or *eustress*, and you can change your attitudes. If you are a worrier, a negative thinker, prone to giving in to depression, and expecting the worst to happen, then you will increase your level of distress. If you think positively, expect good things to happen, learn relaxation techniques, and start exercising, then you will have eustress. Your body will be able to return to a normal, resting state between major stressful incidents. This kind of stress does not have a cumulative effect on the body, such as occurs during distress. In this book I will give you skills you can use to turn your distress to eustress.

How can I tell if I'm a negative thinker?

Unfortunately, many people who have the habit of thinking negatively do not realize they have it. (I know, because I was one of those persons!) A poor self-image is the most common cause for negative thinking. If you would like to determine whether your self-image is negative or positive, answer the following questions:

1. Do I frequently look at others and tell myself I could never be so relaxed or so happy or so in control of my life as they are of theirs?
2. When I undertake something new, do I expect to fail?
3. Could I stop being held back if only other people didn't stand in my way?
4. Do bad things happen to me more often than to other people?
5. Do other people frequently tell me I'm being negative?

If you answered yes to most of these questions and if you also have anxiety at any level, then recognize that you can benefit by learning a new, positive way of looking at yourself. You may not be able to change the circumstances in your life that cause you distress, but you can consciously choose to relate to these circumstances in such a way that they won't control you any longer.

Another Kind of Panic Attack

You have mentioned a poor self-image and "irrational fears" as causes of panic. But the panic I experience is a flashback of a fear that wasn't irrational—my service in the Vietnam war. Do I fit into your definition of a person who has a panic disorder?

Yes. It sounds as if you are suffering from a specific kind of panic disorder which psychologists call Post Traumatic Stress Disorder (PTSD). Vietnam veterans are not the only ones who develop PTSD. Women who have been raped; children who have been emotionally, physically, or sexually abused; anyone who has witnessed a violent crime or bloody accident; and even patients who have undergone disfiguring surgery are subject to it. Some people handle these traumas without developing PTSD because they deal with the horror gradually. Others, like yourself, suppress the trauma, but it doesn't go away. Later, when something happens to remind you of it, you literally erupt with panic, fear, and nightmares. You may feel overcome with guilt and depression.

Although your fear may not have been irrational at the time you witnessed death and destruction in Vietnam, it is certainly irrational to experience panic years later because of it. As with any phobia, you can recover from PTSD through desensitization. You relive the fear-producing events in the presence of others who are supportive. Many Vietnam veterans and rape or incest victims talk their way out of PTSD in support groups made up of other victims who understand and can demonstrate that they care. Others go for one-on-one therapy. By all means, you should seek out such help while you learn to put my Five Basic Principles to work in your life.

But is it really possible to get over a panic disorder completely?

Absolutely. Of the thirteen hundred phobic patients seen at the Phobia Center of the Southwest, in Dallas, over a period of ten years, 75 percent have recovered. These patients function normally. Every year thousands of other people desensitize themselves to their fears and learn new ways of thinking which permit a total cure.

Some people who claim to be recovered agoraphobics will say, "Yes, I can leave my home. I can go shopping. I can go to a restaurant or a party. But I still don't enjoy doing these things. I always have that little bit of fear in the back of my mind that I'm going to have another panic attack." The most these people hope for is to realize that the panic attack isn't going to kill them if it comes and to grit their teeth and make themselves go those places that they must.

A bare minimum existence like this is part of the process of desensitization and a necessary stage for retraining your mind. But it is not the place to get stuck—and that "cure" is *not* the aim of this book.

As I write, I have completed six years without a single twinge of fear that I might have another attack. I have flown to Europe, spoken before audiences of thousands at conventions, and enjoyed myself in the company of friends and business associates wherever I go. I may be tempted to think negatively during a crisis, but I don't. The difference between the way I live and the way a lot of "recovered" agoraphobics exist is that I found a way to keep from giving in to the self-destructive thoughts that lead to anxiety. And by practicing the Five Basic Principles, I don't have to deal with such temptations nearly as often as I used to. Most of the time I feel perfectly comfortable and at ease. I can truthfully report that I feel better than I ever did before I had agoraphobia!

Now I can say that the day I had my first panic attack was the best day of my life. My panic disorder forced me to learn how to use the Five Basic Principles to eliminate negative thinking, build self-confidence, and use the extraordinary powers of my unconscious to eliminate anxiety and panic.

In my opinion, everyone who has a panic disorder can recover as completely as I did. The first step is simply to understand thoroughly how your body and mind work together to produce the fear that causes the terrifying physical symptoms.

CHAPTER 3

~~~~~~

The Rain Barrel Theory

On my first visit to Jim Wilson, I learned how the body, while acting in a perfectly normal way, can cause you to have panic attacks.

"A panic attack is no more than a fight or flight response to sudden danger," Jim explained. "What happens if you suddenly discover that a gigantic grizzly bear has appeared in front of you or that your house is on fire?"

I had to admit I would get pretty frightened under those circumstances.

"Yes, and when you're scared, your heart pounds and your mouth turns dry. Nature provides that you don't have to think about what you should do to respond to your fear. Every defense mechanism within your body is alerted within a fraction of a second. You either fight what threatens you or flee it. You can do these things better and faster because your body is aroused," he said.

"During arousal, the blood vessels in the surface areas of your body constrict so that blood can be diverted deep within to strengthen your muscles. Your heart pounds to rush fuel—oxygen-laden blood—to every cell. Saliva glands dry up in anticipation of the loss of fluids through perspiration. All functions not involved in fighting or fleeing, such as digestion, shut down to conserve energy.

"At this point your body may be so aroused that you don't need any other weapon to fight or flee. But if the brain sees further need, it orders its nuclear warhead—adrenaline. This powerful hormone increases by tenfold all the bodily functions involved in arousal. The result is that you feel an intense panic, an overwhelming, disoriented desire to run. You have superhuman strength to fight or flee."

Negative Thinking Is the Culprit

In my case no frightening specter had appeared to cause my body to produce adrenaline. We figured out that it was my *attitude* toward the stressors in my life that caused me to *sense* danger—even though no real danger existed.

"The body's ability to contain stress is much like a rain barrel that overflows when the water reaches the top," Jim told me. "All of us have rain barrels to contain our stress. As they begin to fill, we start experiencing the sleeplessness and headaches that arousal can cause. When they reach the overflow point, we have serious illnesses like ulcers and heart attacks, or agoraphobia, depending on our body's predisposition."

"But if our bodies have certain predispositions toward disease or panic, wouldn't the cause be genetic or chemical?" I asked.

"Genetics may certainly be involved," he said. He told me about studies done on identical twins which showed that if one had agoraphobia, the other had it too in 40 percent of the cases. If the twins were fraternal, both had agoraphobia in only 5 percent of the cases. And because drugs had been proven to prevent panic attacks, body chemistry was involved, too.

"Ultimately, however, it's your *perception* of the stressors in your life, whether you see them as dangerous or not, that causes your body to produce adrenaline. That's a habit that can be overcome.

"In your case, your mind recognized that your body was so aroused by day-to-day stress that it could no longer ignore what it saw as a great danger. So it put into action the fight or flight response. If you had a more positive attitude, your body would not become so aroused by stressful events," he said.

"I can see why going to the office reminded me of my business problems and raised my stress level," I said. "But what happened at the restaurant, the movies, and the shopping center?"

"Any phobia is an exaggerated and illogical fear reaction to something that shouldn't cause fear at all. You weren't really afraid of those places. You were afraid of the attacks themselves. Whenever you went somewhere you began to worry that you might have another attack. You might pass out as you almost did at your office. Even worse, you might make a fool of yourself in front of others. This anxiety made your rain barrel overflow, and the very thing you feared came to pass once more. You started avoiding more and more places until finally you felt the only safe place for you was your home," he said.

I thought back. My first anxiety attack occurred in the office because my rain barrel happened to overflow there. My second occurred there because returning to the office reminded me of the fear I felt when I had my first attack. Each time I had an attack my fear increased, causing my rain barrel to overflow at new places, which I then avoided. It was a vicious cycle!

"That's right," Jim said. "But you can get over these fears." He urged me to work first on desensitizing myself to my phobia. He told me that I should return to my office. If an attack came, I should realize that my body was just bluffing me. Sure, I had a pounding heart, but I wasn't going to die. I wasn't having a heart attack. When I could go to the office without having an attack, I should start gradually going other places.

The second thing I should do was to start looking at the stressful situations in my life and learn more positive ways of dealing with them. I then told him about the many pressures in my work and my worry about my mother.

"It doesn't matter that you have stress. Everyone does," Jim said. "But you can choose to manage the stress rather than letting it control you."

He recommended that I read several books about how the mind works. One was *Psychocybernetics*, that granddaddy of all self-image books. Maxwell Maltz, a plastic surgeon, described how many patients who had a normal appearance came to him asking to have their faces altered surgically. In their mind's eye, they saw themselves as so ugly that they were willing to undergo the pain and expense of plastic surgery. Yet any mirror would have showed them to be of average, sometimes even better than average, looks. Even more surprisingly, many patients still saw themselves as ugly even after the physician had given them perfectly proportioned features.

How a Poor Self-Image Builds Anxiety

Somehow Maltz's description of the way we distort reality with the vision that we hold of ourselves rang a bell with me. Everyone was always telling me how successful I was. But I didn't see myself that way. I saw myself as a failure, an incompetent, who had six jobs in seven years, who now should be making a lot more money than I was. I viewed myself as a failure as a son who should be able to make his mother feel better than she did. Were these thoughts really valid, or was I, like Maltz's patients, perceiving myself as worse off than I really was? Jim said that by conjuring up visions of danger in my mind I was causing my body to produce panic attacks. My desire to overcome my panic made me willing to admit that I needed to work on creating a better self-image.

I began to realize that even though I had never thought of myself as a negative person, I always did seem to foresee everything that could possibly go wrong. I also spent a lot of time berating myself whenever I didn't finish things I started or do things exactly as I had wished. I now saw that my mind was constantly churning over my limitations and adding more stress to my rain barrel. No wonder it had overflowed!

Another insight I discovered in my study is that our minds don't always know the difference between reality and what we *tell* ourselves is happening. If we tell ourselves we always get the short end of the stick, we will act as if we do, even if the actual facts of the situation would prove otherwise. We are the ones who unwittingly tell ourselves to fail when we are actually in a position to win.

Getting Desensitized

I thought about how I needed to improve my self-image and to script myself for success rather than failure. I started working on that, but I also started trying to desensitize myself. Actually, I had already been trying to go to my office from time to time from dire necessity. I would fill myself full of tranquilizers. When I was completely numb, I would rush to the office, do what I had to do quickly, and then race home. So at Jim's suggestion, I decided I would work on making short trips outside, such as driving myself to a supermarket. Jim told me that if a panic attack came, I was simply to sit quietly in the car until it passed, reassuring myself with the knowledge that I was not going to die. If I sat quietly until the symptoms passed, I could go on with the trip. After each successful trip, I was supposed to go a little farther the next day. I would start out just by driving to the supermarket. Next I would park the car in the supermarket lot and get out. Then I would progress to going to the supermarket door and immediately walking back to the car. Eventually I would go in and fill a shopping basket with groceries. And finally I would be able to shop, wait in line, and pay for the groceries.

Jim also told me I needed to receive lots of positive feedback from my attempts to desensitize myself. He gave me a list of names of other patients who were desensitizing themselves to anxiety. With this list and his words of advice, I planned my first trip.

I was surprised to discover that I really could drive the car four blocks, park in the supermarket lot, and immediately drive home. Of course, I had to fill myself with tranquilizers to do it. My hands became sweaty at the end of the first block. As I went on, my heart began to race, and by the time I arrived, I felt on the verge of blacking out. But I did not get a full-fledged panic attack. I sat quietly in the parking lot and reminded myself I wasn't going to die, that I was just experiencing some bodily arousal, and that at worst I would feel a fight or flight response. I drove back home, walked shakily into my house, and collapsed into a chair. As soon as I was calm, I called one of my fellow-sufferers and reported what I had felt.

"You did great!" he told me. "You're doing just fine."
And that was heady praise!

The next day I repeated my trip. I reminded myself that I had done it yesterday, and I could do it today. I was going to be okay. This time I drove a little farther before my heart began to race.

My progress in desensitizing myself was slow but steady. I was determined that I was going to get over my panic. I was thoroughly committed to the idea, even though I was still very much afraid and I found desensitization hard work.

The Five Basic Principles

Now I know that I could have progressed much faster if I had known and used the Five Basic Principles on which my Five-Point Program is based. They are as follows:

1. Use the creative powers of your unconscious mind to help you change yourself.
2. Use visualizations and affirmations to change your self-image so that you feel confidence rather than fear.
3. Use rational and positive thinking to see yourself and events as they really are and also to visualize how you want them to be.
4. Act *as if* you are already the way you want to be.
5. Set goals to become the person you want to be.

These five principles may seem like just a bunch of words to you right now, but they are powerful. I will be describing them in much greater detail in the next five chapters.

The Haunted House

I'm sure you recall the first time you went into a haunted house at Halloween as a child. Someone was shrieking and moaning. It was pitch black inside. When you put your hand into some gooey stuff, you just knew it was blood, guts, and eyeballs.

If you were to go into a haunted house as an adult, you would laugh about it. You know the blood and guts are cold spaghetti and Jell-O, and the eyeballs are nothing but peeled grapes. What makes the difference? As an adult you have perspective and an understanding of realities. You know how the game is played, and it's not terrifying at all. In fact, it's intriguing and even rather funny.

Your panic is much the same. Without education and understanding, it can be the most terrifying thing you have ever experienced. Once you learn how your mind is creating a haunted house that isn't there by causing your body to produce adrenaline, you don't have to have any more fear. If you have a phobia about going to a restaurant or driving in a car or being around a cat at this time, just remember that you will someday be able to laugh at that fear.

Congratulations! In reading these chapters you have taken the first step toward eliminating your panic: you're armed with knowledge. You know that your fear is caused by allowing your rain barrel to fill with irrational fears. You can reduce the amount of fear you feel by learning to respond to the circumstances of your life in a different way.

CHAPTER 4

The Boss No One Told You About: The First Basic Principle

At the time I was suffering from a panic disorder, I didn't know that I had a boss. I thought that I was self-employed. I ran my own business. I was in control of my life, my relationships with other people, my thoughts. But my panic disorder proved me wrong. I had a boss inside me, one that directed my body to have an anxiety attack, whether I wanted it or not.

That boss was my own unconscious mind. Whatever my unconscious told my body to do—even if it was to release adrenaline and make me miserable—then my body obeyed.

If the unconscious has so much power, then we who are subject to panic need to have it working *for* us rather than *against* us. That is exactly what my First Basic Principle will allow you to do:

The First Basic Principle: Use the creative powers of your unconscious mind to help you change yourself.

In this chapter you will learn how your unconscious works and survey some of the techniques you can use to enlist its powerful aid. When you have learned how to reach this boss, you can use it to help free yourself from the symptoms of panic.

How the Unconscious Works

Your *conscious mind* is the one you use all day long to talk to other people, to read, to work, and to accomplish tasks. You know exactly what is going on in your conscious mind. Your *unconscious mind* is a different breed. Scientists as yet do not know exactly what or where the unconscious is. They only know that it exists. While you are going about your daily business using your conscious mind, the unconscious is storing up information obtained from your feelings. It is listening to what your emotions are saying and how they are handling your internal affairs. Meanwhile, the conscious mind is so busy making rational decisions that it doesn't realize the unconscious is working all the time.

There *are* ways in which the conscious mind can influence the unconscious, but most of us don't know how to use them. We usually aren't even aware of what our unconscious mind is saying. Yet when there is any conflict between the two minds, the *unconscious always wins*, hands down!

To complicate measures further, your unconscious doesn't know the difference between fact and fancy. Like a computer, it retains only the information that you program into it. And it can only interpret this information literally.

When I told Cindy, "Every time I go to the office, I have another attack," my unconscious didn't know that I was simply voicing fears. In its memory banks it stored this information as a fact: every time Bob goes to the office he has another attack. Then, when I approached my office, it was as if I pushed the command button on a computer. My unconscious searched its tapes, found the program, and obediently produced the symptoms of panic in my body. All the while I was consciously telling myself I would *not* be anxious. But my boss was in control!

How to Get Your Boss to Help You

Perhaps you are thinking that a panic disorder is a very idiosyncratic condition. Just because my unconscious worked that way, you say, yours won't. But have you ever told yourself that you're afraid you're going to forget someone's name at a party and find later on that you can't introduce him because you can't recall his name? Have you ever been afraid you won't be able to make that important business presentation as well as you should and then catch a cold on the very day it is scheduled?

When Franklin D. Roosevelt was first inaugurated as president of the United States during the world's worst depression, he proclaimed, "The only thing we have to fear is fear itself." Roosevelt knew intuitively that when people are afraid they don't take business risks. They fear that the economy will be poor, and they act accordingly. He believed that if Americans could get over their fear, they would be able to turn the depression around. Their unconscious would be working *for* them rather than *against* them.

You do have a boss that no one ever told you about, and it does influence you. But consider this: if your unconscious controls you, and you are the one who programs the unconscious, then *you can also program it to make good things happen.*

People program their unconscious every day. Suppose that two realtors are trying to sell homes while the market is down. The first one tells himself that interest rates are too high and no one has money for a down payment. His "boss" takes over, and when he works with a prospective buyer he can't act enthusiastic. No one wants to buy a house or even list property with a realtor who has already given up, and his sales plunge even lower. The second realtor tells himself that the down market offers an opportunity for him to help families who want a home by using creative financing. He tells himself he is offering a real service. His confidence and eagerness are contagious, and he actually finds his sales going up.

Or suppose that two people have cancer. One gives in to depression and hopelessness. The other is inspired to do great deeds. The difference is in what each tells himself about what is going on. His unconscious obeys and produces the result for which it is programmed.

How do the bad tapes that produce such disastrous results become programmed into your unconscious? Some come from childhood. Maybe your mother didn't tell you you were ugly. She only said, "I sure wish you'd gotten your sister's pretty, curly hair." That hurt! Your unconscious took in your wounded feelings and made the decision that you were ugly. Mother said so, and there was nothing you could do about it. But that tape was one you programmed when you were only five years old. If you owned an expensive computer, would you hire a preschooler to program it? Of course not. *Use the person you now are to erase old tapes and reprogram them with more rational conclusions*. You can do this by cognitive restructuring, and I'll show you how in Chapter 6.

A lot of faulty input comes from trying to protect yourself from feelings of failure. The very first time you tried to speak before an audience, maybe you *weren't* a spellbinder. Your inexperience made you feel miserable. You told yourself you just weren't a public speaker and thus spared yourself the insecurity of trying to improve. Now every time you face an audience, your throat closes up and your knees shake. The same thing happens to some people about giving a party, confronting a bully, or telling others they love them. Each time you push the command button by trying to do some things at which you believe you failed, your unconscious orders you to fail again.

The key point to grasp about the boss that nobody ever told you about is that both feelings and behavior are a result of the thoughts you entertain. Furthermore, thoughts are simply *ideas*, not reality. They are programmed into you at an early age because of your parents' actions, the environment in which you lived and matured, and circumstances you now face in your life. *If you choose with the conscious part of your mind to take control over the unconscious, you can completely change those thoughts and reprogram your life*.

Unfortunately, you can't take control by merely saying with your conscious mind, "Okay, I know I'm being negative, so now I'm going to change myself. I'm going to be positive. I'm going to feel superior. I'm going to be a great success."

That is not the best way to get your boss to work for you rather than against you. Remember, he doesn't pay much attention to what your conscious mind says unless you use some very special methods. So the first thing you have to learn is *how* to reach the unconscious level of your mind. Then you can learn the techniques that will allow you to make an impression on your boss.

How I Use the Unconscious

The method of reaching the unconscious that works best for me is a simple one that you can easily teach yourself. It involves learning how to relax and lowering your brain wave cycle rhythm to what is called the *alpha state*. In this state, the electrical impulses in the brain cycle at the rate of about ten cycles per second. This level of brain activity is by no means abnormal since your brain cycles at this rate when you are either on the point of falling asleep or just waking up. When you are "in alpha," you are totally relaxed. You are fully aware of the messages your unconscious is sending to you. At this stage, even more importantly, you can influence your unconscious as well. I'll tell you more about how you can put yourself into the alpha state whenever you want to in Chapter 5.

Once you learn to turn off the conscious mind and reach this meditative state, you can then use special techniques to reprogram your unconscious. These include affirmations and visualizations, which are the heart of the Second Basic Principle.

You may use the techniques of all of the Basic Principles at either the conscious or unconscious level. But when you use them while you are in alpha, you enlist the help of your boss, who will go on working for you even when you are not aware of him. That is why it is so important to learn to use the creative powers of the unconscious mind.

A Quick Look at Affirmations and Visualizations

Because affirmations and visualizations play such an important role in the alpha state, let's stop and take a brief look at what they are.

Affirmations are statements to yourself that you are at this very moment the way you want to be. If you are feeling anxious and depressed, you should affirm the fact that you are perfectly calm, lovable, and worthy. When you affirm while in the alpha state, your unconscious receives the message more easily. It works to put you into a healthier state of mind—and it keeps on doing this even when you are consciously thinking about other things.

Visualizations are the mental pictures you create of yourself accomplishing whatever you want to do or be. You are visualizing when you daydream, but there is a crucial difference in the kind of visualization I use and am teaching you. I am not talking about letting the mind wander wherever it will. I *plan ahead* what I will see. Like a short story, my visualizations have a plot, a theme, and a resolution. In the end, I am different from the way I started out. Since the unconscious believes that what you visualize dramatically is real, you can enlist the aid of your unconscious boss simply by picturing yourself doing things exactly the way you want.

For example, I had tried to improve my golf game for years without success. I read books, watched experts, and practiced what the golf pros told me to do. Regardless, I stayed at the same plateau. After I learned how to visualize, I began to picture myself using the perfect form that I observed in the experts. Every morning when I went into alpha, I spent some time envisioning my hand grip the club and my shoulder going down just so. I fantasized my club face connecting with the ball. Then I happily watched the ball arc into the air, hit the ground, and roll straight toward the hole. When I actually did go to play, I didn't spend a lot of time worrying about whether I was doing everything right. I just played for enjoyment. Six months after I began using visualizations, I had dropped nine strokes off my handicap!

Dr. O. Carl Simonton, a Fort Worth radiation oncologist, advises his patients to visualize the shrinking away of their tumors. Although he makes no claim to be a miracle worker, some cancer patients who had been told by other physicians that they were terminal have experienced remissions. Visualizations can bring about better health, behavior changes, or any improvements you want to make.

Many athletes repeatedly visualize themselves doing perfect gymnastic routines, throwing a flawless curve ball, or doing a winning slalom run. Many coaches of professional sports now require their team members to visualize to sharpen their performance. Of course, you can use visualizations for improvement in other areas besides sports. You can visualize better health and composure under trying circumstances, or whatever you desire.

Using the Unconscious to Desensitize

I first learned to use the unconscious during the period in which I was desensitizing myself to my phobia. What a difference it made! I found that if I went into alpha and visualized and affirmed myself as being perfectly calm and serene in the places that I planned to go, then the actual trip was fairly uneventful.

Since I was still housebound most of the time, I had plenty of time to practice going into alpha and using visualizations and affirmations. Often I would go into alpha six times a day—once in the morning when I woke up, then at midmorning, noon, midafternoon, shortly before supper, and before I went to bed. If I planned to go to a restaurant, I would desensitize myself by going into alpha several times during the two days beforehand. I would visualize myself going inside a restaurant, drinking a glass of water, and leaving. I would also affirm that I was perfectly calm, feeling fine, and enjoying myself.

Right before the time came for me actually to leave the house for the restaurant, I would go into alpha for a booster visualization and affirmation. When I did set foot out of the house and headed for the restaurant, my unconscious evidently believed that I had already made that trip successfully before. I had much less anxiety than I had, for example, when I tried to go to the supermarket without practicing in alpha ahead of time. Within a few days, by using my unconscious, I was able to go to a restaurant and eat a meal without feeling nervous.

Using the Unconscious for Health and Success

I was so pleased with the help my unconscious gave me in desensitizing myself that I started using this new tool to improve my health. For a year and a half before my first panic attack, I had had a spastic colon. Every single day I had a gripping attack. I never got over it. When I programmed myself to be peaceful, lovable, and worthy, however, my unconscious responded. I haven't had a single bout of diarrhea since. It is as if my unconscious just drained my rain barrel, leaving my body and mind in a completely relaxed state.

Does all this sound too good to you? It did to me when I first discovered it. But the truth is, I no longer have to work hard to achieve freedom from panic and anxiety-related problems. My unconscious does it for me.

During the ensuing years I have used my unconscious to improve my business, my personal relationships, and my self-image. If I hadn't had a phobia, I would have simply limped through life, suffering from poor health, constant fears, and self-limiting habits. I would never have had the motivation to learn to relax my body and reprogram my unconscious. That's why I tell every group of agoraphobics to whom I lecture that agoraphobia is the greatest thing that ever happened to me.

A lot of people who come to me for help tell me, "Oh, Bob, I'm too old to change. That's just the way life is. I don't have time to learn all those techniques." Believe me, once you get started, you will see that these techniques are not anything you have to work at. They are something you *want* to do. You will find pleasure spending your time in this way.

Will my techniques work for you? If you have a conscious and unconscious mind, they will. And remember, everyone has both!

CHAPTER 5

~~~~~~

How to Send a Message to Your Boss

When you are able to relax both the body and the mind in special ways, you have access to amazing power to accomplish things that otherwise seem impossible. This is not newly discovered information. It has been known for centuries.

One day, after making a speech before a national convention in New Orleans, I caught a taxi to the airport. The driver, a dark-complexioned man with an unfamiliar accent, asked about my speech. When I told him I had talked about relaxing the mind and body to reduce the stress that leads to panic, he chuckled and held up a book he had been reading. It was about meditation.

"You Americans think that using your mind to control your body is something new. My people have been doing that for a long time," he told me.

"Where are you from?"

"India," he replied. We had a fascinating discussion about Yoga. In the Hindu religion, yogis practice certain moral purifications as well as sexual and dietary abstentions. They learn to stabilize the rhythm of their breathing and deliberately look within themselves rather than without.

The result is that yogis are able to attain an altered state of consciousness that allows them to accomplish what most of us consider to be miracles. Proficient yogis withstand pain, survive while buried underground for hours, and walk on hot coals with no resulting injury. Some even claim that their consciousness can leave the body and return to it.

Scientists did not understand these miracles until they invented the encephalograph and determined the way yogis differed physiologically while they were in an altered state. With this instrument, doctors measured the frequency of the tiny electrical charges that pulsate through all human brains. They found that the number of cycles per second was higher when human beings were awake and active than when they were sleeping. The encephalograph proved that some yogis could remain mentally alert while their brain wave cycle was at the level at which most people fall asleep.

The taxi driver and I agreed that not many Americans, busy with an active life, would spend the years of practice and devotion to Yoga that are required to become a full-fledged yogi, no matter how many miracles they could perform.

"But the good news is that you don't have to do all that," I told him. "Within a day or two you can learn to lower your brain wave activity to the alpha level. When your brain is at alpha, you can tell your unconscious mind what you want to do, and it will make the changes you want in your health, mental condition—even your relationships with other people. Within a short time you may be doing things every bit as miraculous as the most highly sensitive yogis do!''

There are lots of ways to reach such an altered state of consciousness. Many busy Americans practice techniques of relaxation to achieve improvements in their lives. Zen, transcendental meditation, and self-hypnosis are different means to this end. Doctors and psychologists use biofeedback machines that meter patients' heart rate, respiration, temperature, and brain wave activity. Patients teach themselves, by hit-or-miss practice while hooked up to these machines, to lower their brain wave frequency and then command their bodies to attain better health.

Some people who run achieve an altered state of consciousness, but what I am talking about is different from the runner's high experienced by aerobic athletes. Hundreds of thousands of people in many countries have already learned to relax and go into the alpha state as I do and then program themselves for changes they want.

I am going to show you how you can easily reach the alpha state, too, but first let's examine the different levels of consciousness.

Brain Cycles and States of Consciousness

The encephalograph proves that we all experience several different states of consciousness every day. We are wide awake and alert, for instance. Or we are quiet and intuitive. Or we are asleep. Physiologically, these states are defined by the rate at which the brain waves are cycling. Scientists have identified four primary states:

- beta, when the brain registers fourteen or more cycles per second (CPS),
- alpha, when it registers seven to fourteen CPS,

- theta, when it registers four to seven CPS, and
- delta, when it registers below four CPS.

The state which most of us are in up to 80 percent of our time is beta, the state of the conscious mind. Scientists also know that while we are in beta, our left brain dominates. The left brain is responsible for rational thought—the ability to speak, to work mathematical problems, to organize thoughts, and to compare past experiences with the present. At beta, you are wide awake, alert, aware of all five of your senses, and making decisions. You can learn, study, and work. When you are highly excited or agitated, your brain may register as high as sixty CPS, but you are still in beta.

Alpha is the creative state. When you dream, or when you are relaxed or drowsy yet aware, you are in alpha. You may not notice what your eyes, ears, nose, and sense of touch are telling you, yet you have a feeling of passive awareness.

Scientists know that the right brain dominates at alpha. It is intuitive rather than rational. With it, you think in images and detect patterns. Although you don't have the active control over speech and rational thought that you have while you are in beta, you have something even better. You can receive solutions to problems in a single flash rather than plodding through the left brain's maze of logic to find them.

The alpha state is the one I want to teach you to reach on demand. At this level you can contact the boss, which either makes your life miserable and anxious or, if you control him, works to solve your problems for you.

At the theta level, most people fall asleep. With practice, however, you can learn to remain passively aware as do very accomplished yogis. The theta state gives yogis their extraordinary powers of physical control and extrasensory perception, their deep tranquillity and euphoria. If you were able to program your unconscious while you were in the theta state, overcoming panic would be even simpler. I have been able to achieve a full recovery from a severe panic disorder simply by reprogramming at alpha.

At delta, everyone is in a deep sleep state and has total unawareness.

How Does the Alpha State Feel?

Again, let me emphasize that all of us pass through these four stages of consciousness every day. Nothing is mysterious or foreign or dangerous about the alpha state. *You have been in the alpha state at some point every day of your life.*

The best way to realize what the alpha state feels like is to think about the moments right before you drop off to sleep. Do you sometimes get such good ideas that you tell yourself, "I must remember this"? If so, you are in alpha. Or think back to the way you feel when you first wake up in the morning and haven't yet gotten out of bed. Do creative thoughts and solutions to your problems flood your mind? If you don't write down these flashes of insight, you are likely to forget them. Once the left brain takes over in the beta state, your mind is wholly involved with the information your five senses continuously feed you.

You can also be in alpha whenever you are practicing meditation or self-hypnosis, reflecting quietly with your eyes closed, daydreaming, or even when you are praying.

After I took a course to learn how to reach the alpha state, I realized that I had already been putting myself into alpha without realizing it. I had been spending hours reading self-help books after seeing Jim Wilson. Alone in the house, I would be quiet and relaxed. Often I would lay the books aside to reflect deeply on them. I now am sure that when I did, I was in the alpha state. Just being in alpha helped reduce my anxiety and panic. After all, you can't be anxious and relaxed at the same time.

I also stumbled onto a way to go one step further and contact my unconscious. As I read books on positive thinking, I reflected on them by repeating some of the strong affirmations I read in them. I frequently told myself I was feeling calmer and happier as these books advised, even though I didn't believe it. Now I am sure that those affirmations I made while in a natural state of alpha had an effect. I happened onto a way to reprogram myself. How much better, however, it is to be able to reach the alpha state on demand several times a day! How much more effective it is to plan *deliberately* to control the boss within with proven techniques.

How to Reach the Alpha State

The *Alpha Script* which I am going to give you will enable you to reach the alpha state the very first time you try. You may have someone read it to you as you relax with your eyes closed. Or better still, tape record the script in your own voice and play it back.

Some preparations are necessary. First, find a quiet spot where you will not be interrupted by noise, distractions, or other people. Make yourself as comfortable as possible. You may sit upright with your feet on the floor and your hands in your lap with your palms up. Or you may lie on your back with your arms parallel to your body. Whichever position you choose, remember to close your eyes, avoid crossing your legs, and make sure that your spine is straight. You should feel comfortably balanced.

The first step in the script is to teach your body what it

feels like to relax. You do this by tensing your muscles as tightly as you can, using all your strength, and then letting them go loose. The difference between the tension you feel when you have stressed your muscles and the calm you feel upon loosening them gives you a reference point for the feeling of relaxation. The script calls for you to tighten and relax all your muscles, beginning with your head and following with all the parts of your body.

A word of advice here: if any muscle group hurts when you tighten it, avoid further tightening. The goal is to achieve relaxation, and pain can only make you feel more tense.

The next step in the script is deep breathing. You start out by deliberately concentrating on how your breath goes in and out. The goal is to breathe with your diaphragm, just as a sleeping baby does. Your whole stomach area should move up and down. You can tell if you are breathing deeply enough by placing your hand on your stomach. If your abdomen pushes your hand out while you are breathing in, you are breathing correctly. The reason you should breathe deeply is that many anxious people get in the habit of breathing shallowly, from the chest up. Or they breathe in irregular fashion from the mouth. In normal breathing, the oxygen that you breathe in is perfectly balanced with the carbon dioxide that you breathe out. You maintain an acid-alkaline balance, or pH level, as it is called, in the blood. When you breathe shallowly, you breathe out carbon dioxide but don't breathe in enough oxygen. An unbalanced pH level is just one more bucketful of stress that can make your rain barrel overflow. You can't relax if you are not breathing properly, so you need to use the total capacity of your lungs, holding the air for a while and then breathing it all out. By doing this you allow the lungs to extract more oxygen from the air and put it into the bloodstream.

Also, concentrating on the rhythm of your breathing causes you to let go of distracting thoughts that might prevent you from lowering your CPS level.

A Very Important Visualization

Next you will need to practice one very important visualization to reach the alpha state. I call this visualization your *secret resting place*, because everyone creates a different visualization. You should choose the most relaxing place you have ever been and picture it vividly in your mind. Perhaps you used to fish in a beautiful mountain stream or lie beside a quiet lakeside on a calm day or float on an inner tube in a tranquil pool. You may have swayed in a childhood swing or snuggled into a feather mattress in the security of your grandmother's house.

As you prepare to go into alpha, take a few moments and use the following six steps to perfect your visualization of your secret resting place.

1. Close your eyes and look at the scene. Seek out all the details.
2. What color are the trees, the sky, the clouds, the water? See your scene in living color.
3. Are there any sounds in your secret resting place? Can you hear the water roar, lap, swish? Are birds singing? Does the swing creak? Listen to them.
4. What do you feel in your secret resting place? Is the water warm or cool? Is the feather mattress slightly lumpy, and are the sheets smooth or rough? Is the ground you are lying on sandy or grassy? Feel the sensations.
5. Are there any smells of honeysuckle or moss in your secret resting place? The rubber of the inner

tube? The slight odor of feathers in the mattress? Smell the odors.

6. What do you look like in your visualization? Are you smiling, is your face calm and serene, is your body relaxed? If you can't see yourself, imagine that you are looking at the scene on a movie screen and seeing yourself in it.

These are ways you can make your visualization more effective. If you cannot see the scene clearly, do not strain. At first you may have to aim for the feelings, smells, and sounds. Do not worry if your scene doesn't stay in focus at first. You will get better at visualizing as you go along, and the fun part is that you can change things so the scene is exactly as you like it!

The Countdown

Going into alpha once you have relaxed is a simple matter of counting yourself down from ten to one. When you have reached alpha, you will go to your secret resting place for a few moments. (And undoubtedly you will want to stay there for the sheer enjoyment of it. Take a mental picture of the wonderful feeling of peace you have there so that you can bring it up later when you are feeling tense.) While you are at your secret resting place, your senses will be alert. You will know what is going on around you, but you will be able to concentrate totally on the thoughts that are coming, unbidden, into your mind. If the thoughts that come happen to be negative, fearful, or anxious, do not try to control them; you will only force yourself back into beta as you make use of your rational mind. Simply accept that it is okay to have these thoughts and gently push them away by enjoying the sights, sounds, smells, and peace of your resting place.

When you want to leave the alpha level, the process is simple. You count yourself up slowly to the beta level. You let go of your secret resting place, open your eyes, and find yourself in beta because you tell your unconscious that that is what you will do.

The Alpha Script

Below is the script that will help you learn to reach the alpha level. Eventually you will be able to go into alpha quite easily without using the script.

I suggest that you read it through carefully. But don't try to go into alpha while reading it. You can't. While you read, you are in the beta state. When you are ready to go to alpha, either have someone read this script to you or tape record it and play it back to yourself:

You are feeling very comfortable, very quiet, very calm and peaceful, and soon you will be going into alpha, a normal, creative level of the mind.

Now you will begin to tighten your muscles to the count of four, clenching them as tightly as possible and holding them tensed to the count of four, then releasing them to the count of four. Starting with your head and shoulders, you are now tightening the muscles in your face, jaw, neck, and shoulders. Study the tension. Become aware of what it feels like so you will be able to recognize it when you are awake. One, two, three, four. *(The counting period should last a total of five to seven seconds.)* Hold, two, three, four. Now release these muscles, two, three, four. Tighten, two, three, four; hold, two, three, four; release, two, three, four. Tighten, two, three, four; hold, two, three, four; release, two, three, four. Tighten, two, three, four; hold, two, three, four; release, two, three, four. Become aware of the relaxation as you let go.

You will now tighten the muscles in your hands by making a fist. Tighten, two, three, four; hold, two, three, four; release, two, three, four. *(Repeat four times.)*

You will now tighten the muscles in your arms, making them as stiff and rigid as you can. Curl your arms up as you would when you flex your arm muscles. Tighten, two, three, four; hold, two, three, four; release, two, three, four. *(Repeat four times.)*

You will now tighten the muscles in your chest and abdomen. Tighten, two, three, four; hold, two, three, four; release, two, three, four. *(Repeat four times.)*

You will now tighten the muscles in your pelvis and buttocks area. Tighten, two, three, four; hold, two, three, four; release, two, three, four. *(Repeat four times.)*

You will now tighten the muscles in your feet and toes. Tighten, two, three, four; hold, two, three, four; release, two, three, four. *(Repeat four times.)*

You will now tighten the muscles in your legs. Tighten, two, three, four; hold, two, three, four; release, two, three, four. *(Repeat four times.)*

Always notice what it feels like when you let go. You are now feeling very calm and rested, in complete control. You are feeling relaxed and fine.

You will now begin to do deep breathing. You will breathe in through your nose and out through your mouth. You will let your stomach rise as you inhale as deeply as possible to the count of four. As you exhale to the count of four you will completely empty the contents of your lungs and let your stomach drop. Your lungs are now filling in the lower part of your abdomen, one; in your chest area, two; up, up, up, three, four. Hold your breath, two, three, four; exhale, two, three, four. Each time you breathe in, your body will become heavier and heavier. Again concentrate on letting go all over your body. *(Repeat four more times.)*

Now you will picture your body as being totally relaxed. Imagine that you are like a limp rubber doll, in which the rubber is all stretched out and the stuffing is gone. Imagine your scalp is becoming loose and tingly. The rubber of your scalp is so loose and pliable that it sags down on your forehead. The skin of your face sags around your eyes. A soft, gentle breeze caresses your face, and it feels very good. Allow your mouth to droop like a rubber mask. Now your jaw has completely dropped and you are releasing all tensions there.

Imagine that your arms are like rubber. They are hanging limply from your shoulders. Your torso is so limp that it hangs on your spine. Your legs are like rubber bands, dangling from your hips. Your feet are detached from your body, connected only by a thread.

Imagine that you are floating in a warm, sparkling liquid. You are completely relaxed and in control of your mind and body. You are at a deeper, healthier level of the mind. Yet you are feeling aware and can function exactly as you wish.

To enter a deeper, healthier level of the mind, imagine that you are going down a staircase. With each step down you are becoming more and more relaxed. Count backward from ten to one as you go down the stairs. Ten, nine, eight, seven, six, five, four, three, two, one. You are feeling fine and are using your improved mental faculties to help yourself and others. You are perfectly relaxed, completely calm, and in a moment you will be going to your secret resting place. You will count backward from three to one, and at the count of one you will be in your secret resting place, enjoying the calm, the quiet, the peace, the joy. Three, two, one.

(Allow five minutes of silence at this point.)

You are now completely in control of your thoughts. You are feeling rested and relaxed.

You are now going to count from one to five, and at the count of five, you will open your eyes, be wide awake, feeling fine, and in perfect health. You will be feeling better and better. One, two, coming up slowly, slowly; three, at the count of five you will be opening your eyes, wide awake, feeling fine, and in perfect health, four . . . five. Say, "I am wide awake, feeling fine, and in perfect health."

Yes, You Were in Alpha!

Did you enjoy your deep relaxation and your trip into alpha? I am always surprised at the varying reactions people have to the first time they use this script.

"I never felt so good," some say. Others are disappointed. "I didn't feel any different than I ever did," they report. Some even complain. "I wasn't at alpha. I could have sat up and done anything I wanted to right in the middle of the script."

All of these reactions are the way you are supposed to feel. You don't feel different, because you have been in the alpha state countless times before. *You* are in control of your own mind; no one else is. Some people slip into theta and sleep before the script is through. That's all right, too. If you reach the theta state, it's a sure sign that you made it to alpha on the way! If you continue working with the script, you will stop falling asleep and learn to maintain yourself in alpha.

Even if you're not sure that you reached the alpha state, you undoubtedly did. At this point, all you have to do is to follow the script. You will feel fine, better than before, and more calm for having followed it.

Of course, you could prove to yourself that you had reached alpha if you were hooked up to a biofeedback machine. You would see that your brain waves were cycling at the rate of ten to fourteen CPS as you listened to the script. But the important thing is not to worry about whether you did reach that level or not. Just be assured that if you keep on relaxing and practicing with the script, you *will* be in alpha.

Once you start seeing some results of programming yourself as you use the script, you will know that you reached alpha even though you didn't feel any different. After becoming convinced, you will then begin to recognize that the feeling of passive calmness that comes to you while listening to the script is the same feeling you have when you first wake up and are in alpha naturally.

As a matter of fact, I wasn't sure that I was in alpha the first few times I tried to reach that state. But I kept on. Soon I was feeling such a wonderful sense of peace and freedom from tension that I realized I had never really known how to relax before. I had never been able to avoid the constant bracing that led to such havoc in my mind and body. While I was in alpha, I gained a tremendous awareness that for most of my life I had been in a state of anxiety and worry. Now for the period that I was in alpha, I was free of it.

For a confirmed cynic like myself to believe that an internal boss could be ordered to work miracles was even more difficult. You can program some simple results early on as a proof that you can influence your unconscious while in alpha. For instance, you can tell yourself while you are in your secret resting place that in the night you will wake up and remember your dreams. Or you can tell yourself that you will wake up at the time you want to arise the next morning without the use of an alarm clock.

Cindy and I did just that the first evening we tried to go into alpha. We were skeptical, but before we went to bed we gathered up pencil and paper for writing down the dreams, and we shut off the alarm clock. To our surprise, we each woke up several different times and recorded our dreams. This was the first time that Cindy had been able to remember a dream in a long time. And when 7:00 A.M. arrived, we both woke up, right on the button. We began to believe that we were in alpha and that we were really influencing our boss.

After that, I began to take myself into alpha many times a day. Other than the above experiments which I used to prove that I was in alpha, I did not attempt to program my unconscious during the first week. I simply enjoyed the wonderful peace that this state of relaxation brought. While I was in my secret resting place, I just rested. But I was appalled at some of the thoughts that came unbidden into my mind. Still filled with fear and anxiety in those days, my unconscious told me about suicide and murder. It sent irrational, crazy, angry thoughts into my mind. I learned that the best thing to do was not to resist them, but to recognize them as being my unconscious thoughts. Then they would flow out of me.

It helped to remember that even though these thoughts seemed bizarre, they were just thoughts, not actions. By reaching my boss and giving him directions, I could change them. In fact, these thoughts gave me a good picture of what I needed to change. My unconscious was letting me know that I thought I was not good enough, that I was inferior and a fraud.

Using this self-knowledge, I wrote out a new goal. Previously I had thought my first priority should be to use my boss to help me overcome my panic attacks. But now I saw how difficult a task this would be if I continued to feel about myself the way my unconscious told me I did. So I resolved to continue working on the desensitization. But I would make my number one goal that of changing my self-image. I felt calmer just knowing that my unconscious was going to help me see myself as a loving and good person, full of self-worth.

Your First Week's Program

Here's what you should do during the first week you are learning to go into alpha:

1. If your panic disorder is so severe that you are housebound, plan to use the script six times a day. Start before breakfast, then use it again at midmorning, before lunch, at midafternoon, before supper, and before going to bed. If your problem is not as critical, you can get by by using the script only three times a day—upon arising, before lunch, and before you go to bed. Even if you hold a full-time job, you should make an attempt to use the script at midday or during a coffee break. Find some place you can be alone for a few minutes and use the script. If that's impossible, you can at least do the relaxation and deep breathing part in the restroom!
2. Don't try to challenge any thoughts that come to your mind while you are relaxing in your secret resting place. Just recognize that they are there. It's okay to have them. Nudge them away by enjoying the sights, sounds, smells, and peace in your resting place.
3. Note the feelings you have when you first wake

up and right before you go to sleep and compare them with the feelings you have while you use the Alpha Script.

4. Also note the feeling of muscle relaxation that you achieve after doing the tensing and relaxing in the script. Teach your body to let go like that every time you feel tense during the day. Eventually you will no longer need to do muscle tensing to reach the alpha state. Your body will know what the state of relaxation feels like.

5. Go to an office supply store and buy a supply of blue dot stickers. Place blue dots any place where you are apt to feel nervous. You could stick a blue dot on the dashboard of your car, the front of your typewriter, or at the kitchen sink, for instance. Whenever your eye falls on the blue dot, ask yourself if you are feeling tension. If you are, consciously seek to relax your muscles. If you have time and privacy, you can use the script and actually go into alpha to get over the tension. Or you can simply use this blue dot strategy as a way of discovering what makes you tense.

6. Don't worry about whether you are really reaching the alpha state or not. Just keep on practicing. Don't push or strain. Know that you are doing something very good for your body and for your peace of mind.

7. If unbidden thoughts persist while you are in your secret resting place, take some time during the day to write out the way you would like to change those thoughts to be different from what the thoughts are telling you. Don't try to do anything about these thoughts yet. Save what you have written for use later on.

CHAPTER 6

~~~~~~

Putting Visualizations and Affirmations to Work: The Second Basic Principle

In the last chapter you mastered the First Basic Principle. You are now able to go into alpha whenever you want to with or without the Alpha Script. You can enjoy the feeling of relaxation and peace that being in alpha brings to you. In this chapter you will learn how to use two very important tools—visualizations and affirmations. With these tools you can reprogram your unconscious boss.

Second Basic Principle: Use visualizations and affirmations to change your self-image so that you feel confidence rather than fear.

The Alpha Script has made you somewhat familiar with the tools of visualization and affirmation. Using the script, you visualized your secret resting place and recreated a scene in your mind that you had experienced before. By remembering the scene with all five of your senses, you enabled your boss to send you feelings of calmness and peace.

You also used at least one strong affirmation at the close of the Alpha Script. You said, "I am wide awake, feeling fine, and in perfect health." This positive statement which you made about yourself helped reinforce the peaceful feelings evoked by the visualization.

You are now ready to learn how to visualize scenes that have not yet happened and to affirm that you are already different from the way you now are.

Alex, a successful young contractor, used visualizations and affirmations in this way to overcome the panic symptoms he developed whenever he found himself in a crowd. Alex frequently entertained business associates by inviting them to attend the football games for which he owned a bloc of tickets. Then one day Alex began to feel dizzy whenever he entered the domed stadium filled with thousands of people. Somehow he felt a gripping, irrational fear that the ceiling was going to fall on him. For no explainable reason, the noise, the packed bodies around him, the long flights of stairs, and the lights made him so jittery he could scarcely breathe. Soon Alex began to avoid going to the games, even though he knew his clients wondered why he no longer provided the enjoyable freebies. He was so afraid that he would lose control in a crowd that he didn't try to initiate any other form of business entertainment, even though he knew he ran the risk of losing clients in this way.

Finally Alex learned to visualize himself as being calm at the football games. He pictured himself smiling and laughing as he and the other men watched the game. He affirmed, "I enjoy being with my clients at the game. I feel calm and happy." He practiced these visualizations and affirmations at alpha daily and right before he set out to go to the stadium. While he watched the game, he repeated the affirmation again. Using these tools, Alex got over his panicky symptoms. Now he entertains his business associates and friends at the football games with no problems whatsoever.

How Visualizing and Affirming Work

Perhaps you think that imagining scenes and telling yourself things about yourself that really aren't true are a denial of fact. As a matter of fact, nature provides ways for us to do the very same thing when we daydream.

Just think back to your favorite daydream. It doesn't matter how unrealistic it is. You might fantasize that you're the first person to command a spaceship to planet Z in another galaxy, or that you've just been elected president of the United States by a landslide, or that you have received kudos for playing the lead part in the latest Broadway hit. Close your eyes, sit, and replay your favorite daydream for a few minutes before you read on.

Now how do you feel? Euphoric? Have you temporarily forgotten any worries or bodily discomfort that usually bother you? Do you have the feeling that you can conquer any problem that presents itself? Daydreams allow you to lose all sense of time and place, much as you do when you are at alpha in your secret resting place. After you stop daydreaming, you are left with all the happy emotions you might have if you had actually been the first person on planet Z or won a presidential election or received accolades for your opening night performance.

Why does this happen? Because when you are daydreaming, you are in alpha and you are programming your unconscious boss to send you these positive emotions.

Though you may not have thought of it before, *you have been using visualizations and affirmations to send commands to your unconscious all your life*. All of us constantly think in vivid, deeply felt pictures, and we continually chatter silently to ourselves. What we picture and say to ourselves affects the way we feel emotionally and physically. If your mental pictures are positive and happy, then you feel upbeat and able to achieve much more than you normally can. If your mental pictures and mind chatter are negative, then you feel depressed or nervous, causing your rain barrel to fill with anxiety. The result can be panic or health problems.

The mental pictures and mind chatter we create can affect our emotional health as much as our actions and physical well-being. For instance, let's look at two women who buy themselves the same new dress and expect to look good in it. The different mental pictures and messages they create can cause them to have radically different feelings.

Marcia looks in the mirror of the dressing room and says, "I look great." She can just "see" the smile on her boyfriend's face when she wears it for their next date. When she actually does meet her boyfriend, she is so radiant and charming that he can't help but like the way she looks in the new dress. Marcia's ability to relax and be charming is a result of her visualization and affirmation in the dressing room, which made her unconscious boss believe that she had *already received a compliment* from her boyfriend. Since she feels emotionally attached to her boyfriend, the effectiveness of her mind pictures and messages is heightened. The resulting feelings of self-esteem permit her to be at her best on the date.

Jan buys the same dress. As she tries it on, she tells herself, "I look great." But at the same time she worries about overspending the budget. She pictures her husband's angry face and tells herself, "I'm going to get in trouble."

Sure enough, her boss takes in the negative visualization and mental message and makes her nervous and panicky when she wears the dress. Her husband can't see that she looks great. All he sees is a fidgety, anxious person who, through her body language, tells him he is justified in becoming angry.

Why You Should Take Control of Your Visualizations and Affirmations

Let's look at the visualizations and mental chatter most of us use to see how we, like Jan, command our unconscious boss to create problems for us. Let's say you have been invited to a business cocktail party where you have the opportunity to make a crucial contact. You know it's important to come across well. But while you stand and chat with that important person, your mind is paying no attention to what you are saying. Instead, it is focusing on one of your own self-limiting beliefs, such as that you aren't good enough to be taking up this rich, important person's time.

As you talk to Mr. Powerful, your mind is picturing your poor self-image in every wretched detail. Your boss sees your negative visualization, receives the command, and sets out to make you feel inferior. He makes your smile look forced and your laughter nervous.

And what is your mind *telling* you as you sip your drink? "No one here really wants to listen to me. I know I'm boring. I'm not assertive like Bill, not as attractive as Diane. How much longer do I have to endure this torture?" "Torture" and "endure" are negative mental messages, the very opposite of an affirmation to your boss. You are programming him to make you seem boring and unattractive.

Most of us worry, and some of us do it almost all the time. We daydream by the hour, picturing negative outcomes to future events. We embellish our fear that we will fail or that we'll make a mistake or that we'll be embarrassed. Because worry involves such strong emotions, it is the most potent command to the unconscious.

Since it is so easy to affect your unconscious by mental imagery and mind chatter, why not opt for the best? That's what the October 1984 issue of *Alive* magazine (published by the Shaklee Corporation) reported that Luis Tonizzo did when he competed in the 1984 Royal Western/*Observer* Singlehanded Race (OSTAR). In this sailing event, the competitors and their boats face the dangers of the Atlantic Ocean alone in a three-thousand-mile voyage from Plymouth, England, to Newport, Rhode Island. This open-water sailing race is known as the most perilous one in the world.

For six months before the race, Tonizzo underwent a heavy physical training program, took cold showers to prepare himself for icy, wet weather, and built up his body with dietary supplements. But he went one step farther than most of the participants. As part of his training, he visualized exactly how he would cope with each emergency that might occur. When the time came to face icebergs and gales, his unconscious had the feeling he had already overcome these hazards. The situations felt familiar, and he performed as he wished. After twenty days, twenty-three hours, and forty minutes at sea, Tonizzo finished first in his class. When I mastered my Second Basic Principle, I was able to overcome lots of hazards in my own life, too.

My Five-Day Visualization Program

You can easily learn to visualize and affirm as I did within five days if you follow the program I outline for you below.

Day One: Take a lemon. Hold it in your hands. Smell it. Feel its rough texture and elliptical shape. Enjoy its bright, yellow color. Then go into alpha to your secret resting place. Rather than merely letting thoughts come unbidden to your mind, say, "I see the lemon in my mind, and I enjoy creating a mental picture of it." Then picture its elliptical shape. Visualize your hand on it, and as you do, feel its rough texture. Imagine that you are biting into the lemon and tasting the bitter skin and sour juice. Don't be surprised if you start salivating at this point. Your fantasy will evoke a physical response.

If you are unable to visualize the lemon, don't worry. Go back to beta and examine the lemon again. Return to alpha and affirm that you see the lemon, feel its roughness, see its yellow color, and taste its sourness. It may help you to tape instructions to yourself so that you can follow the directions without thinking, just as you did with the Alpha Script.

Practice the visualization and affirmation of your ability to see the lemon each time you go into alpha on Day One.

Day Two: You will now go to alpha and recreate a mental picture of a beautiful red rose. Affirm, "I see a beautiful red rose. I enjoy creating mental pictures of roses." Now see the rose's velvet petals, damp with dew. Examine how each petal fits into the blossom, overlapping the other petals. Notice the yellow center. Feel the sharp thorns on the stem. Put the rose to your nose and smell it.

You will probably be able to see the rose easily. But if

you can't, remember a pleasant time when you actually did hold a rose in your hand. Perhaps you received a red rose at a dance, or your mother had a rose bush that bloomed every spring, or you once went to a flower show or a formal garden and admired the roses. In your mind, actively picture yourself walking up to one of these roses. Pick a single rose and begin your visualization.

Each time you go into alpha on Day Two, practice your visualization of the rose.

Day Three: Go into alpha and see the face of someone you love while that person is the happiest you have ever seen him or her. Affirm, "I am recreating the face of _____ and he (she) is very happy because _____ . I enjoy picturing the face of _____ ." Now see that person's eyes, nose, mouth, and hair. Notice the smile and the look of being fully alive that radiates from the eyes.

Each time you go into alpha on Day Three, visualize this person and affirm that you enjoy doing so.

Day Four: Go into alpha and recreate an entire scene in which there are other people besides yourself. Choose a place where you felt happy and secure, yet excited, too. You might be with a group of tourists on your first visit to one of the famous places of the world. Fantasize the expressions on the faces of your tour companions as they catch a first glimpse of the Eiffel Tower, the Grand Canyon, the Taj Mahal, or a San Francisco cable car. Note the ways each face reflects excitement and joy. See what clothes the people are wearing. What color is the sky? Is the weather rainy or sunny? Are there smells or sounds in the air? Make your visualization as detailed as you possibly can. Tell yourself, "I enjoy recreating the scene at _____ , and I feel exhilarated because I am there."

Each time you go into alpha on Day Four, recreate this same scene.

Day Five: Go into alpha and see yourself. Affirm, "I am recreating my own face. I am in control of my mind and can see myself in every detail. I enjoy picturing my face." Then look at your eyes, nose, mouth, and hair, much as you visualized a person you loved on Day Three. Be sure to see yourself in a happy mood.

If you have trouble visualizing your face, it may help if you first look at yourself in a family movie or videotape. Even a series of snapshots of yourself doing different things can help. When you go into alpha, visualize a huge movie screen. Then put your family movie or snapshot up on the screen.

I admit that I had a problem seeing myself in a scene. I overcame that problem by recreating actual events in my life that had made me very happy. One of the most exciting and happy times I could remember was my high school graduation, and fortunately my mother had home movies of me and my best friend in our caps and gowns which I could view for inspiration. Just looking at the movies brought back the feelings I had had. I was a typical adolescent rebel. That formal graduation ceremony on the high school stage was as exciting as if I'd just been let out of jail!

When I went into alpha, I first visualized the scene. I saw the whole class, each member wearing a cap and gown, sitting on the stage. I could smell the dust from the stage's velvet curtain and hear the creaking of the folding chairs on which we sat, the coughing in the audience, and the principal's voice as he called out each name. I heard the girl who sat next to me giggle and whisper, and I watched my best friend go across the stage as I snickered.

After I had a good look at the whole scene, I zeroed in on my face like a zoom camera. It looked just like the face I saw in the family movie—a big, defiant grin and a look of jubilation in my eyes. I could really see myself and feel the emotions!

Using events like these that are filled with vivid and positive emotions is a good way to help you visualize yourself. I know one man who couldn't picture his own face until he recreated the company meeting at which he received an award. Fortunately, he had a photo of himself being presented the plaque which he could study before going into alpha.

A young woman I was helping couldn't see her face no matter how hard she tried. Finally, she placed a full-length mirror next to her TV. As she watched a comedy, she glanced into the mirror from time to time to capture her expressions as she reacted to amusing scenes and love sequences. Then when she went into alpha, she recreated her face as she saw herself in the mirror.

The Importance of Affirmations

You can use affirmations to overcome specific problems. For instance, you can blot out negative mind chatter such as "Whenever I'm in the supermarket, I begin to feel nervous" with "I enjoy going to the supermarket. I feel perfectly calm and happy." Even though you are in beta, your unconscious boss gets his instructions to send you into panic from the emotionally charged things you are saying to yourself. If you tell yourself you are calm, the level of your rain barrel remains low.

As you can see from this example, you can use affirmation either at beta or alpha. When you use them at beta, however, you are simply *coping with an emergency*. When you use them at alpha, you are reprogramming your unconscious and making a real and permanent change in yourself. That's why I feel so strongly that it is important to go into alpha several times daily and affirm that you are calm and happy. Then you can avoid emergencies entirely.

People have used affirmations in both alpha and beta with good effects for centuries. William James, the great nineteenth-century psychologist and philosopher, wrote: "Believe that life is worth living and your belief will help create the fact." James adopted this philosophy while dealing with an experience that anyone who has ever had a panic disorder can identify with. While studying medicine, he suffered a breakdown that brought on thoughts of suicide. After he received his M.D. degree from Harvard in 1869, he was unable to begin practicing medicine because he had what was then called a phobic panic. For three years he lived in a state of semi-invalidism in his father's house, doing nothing but reading and writing an occasional review.

According to his own statement, James relieved his panic by reading Charles Renouvier, a Kantian Idealist who believed in free will. He wrote: "My first act of free will shall be to believe in free will." With that strong affirmation he abandoned all determinisms in his life—the scientific kind that seemed to have had some relation to his neurosis, for one. In other words, in spite of the current scientific thinking of his time, which gave him little hope for recovery, James affirmed that he had the power to make himself well. And he did cure himself. He went on to travel, lecture, and become an internationally known figure.

James may not have termed his statements about free will "affirmations," but when he told himself he believed that he could be well again, he undoubtedly sent strong messages to his unconscious, which in turn helped free him from his panic.

Where does our unconscious get its opinion about whether our life is worth living or not? One way is from the thoughts that most of us repeat over and over to ourselves about what is going on in our lives. These thoughts come to us unbidden whether we are in beta or alpha. Most of us have a lot of irrational beliefs that come from our childhood, a time when we could not judge events around us in their true light. My belief that I could not participate in sports because of my slightly withered leg and therefore wasn't as good as the other boys is an excellent example. This negative thought grew until it encompassed many areas of my life completely unrelated to sports. We can change such poor self-images by repeating strong, positive thoughts about ourselves to ourselves. Eventually we can replace irrational thoughts.

Here are some examples of good general affirmations that would help anyone subject to anxiety:

1. I am a loving, caring person who deserves success.
2. Every day, in every way, I am becoming the person I want to be.
3. I am perfectly confident, calm, and happy.
4. My body is perfectly healthy and normal.
5. My mind is functioning perfectly, and I am finding new creative ways to live.

These are good affirmations to use at beta to cope with an emergency. Use them when you are in a crowd and feeling nervous or just as you stand up to make a business presentation or step forward to meet an important person or move to the podium to make a speech. Better still, use them at alpha before you do any of those things and make permanent changes in your self-image.

It is even more effective if you tailor your affirmations to the specific problems you want to alleviate. Tell yourself, ''I feel perfectly calm and happy when I am in a crowd at the shopping mall." Or, "My mind is functioning perfectly as I give my business presentation. I am well prepared and I deserve success." Or, "I am a loving, caring person who enjoys meeting new people." Or, "I am perfectly happy that I am making a speech."

Creating Your Own Affirmations

You can create specific affirmations that will help you overcome more personal problems. Go back to the notes you made about the unbidden thoughts that came into your mind while you were in your secret resting place as you practiced with the Alpha Script. When I found unbidden thoughts telling me to commit suicide, I quickly affirmed, "My life has many positives in it. I want to live and enjoy all the good things in my life." When I felt myself becoming overwhelmed with a sense of guilt, I told myself, "I can find a way to make amends if I have really harmed someone. I will love myself and look to the future."

Creating your own affirmations is really very simple and a fast way to help yourself overcome anxiety. Just remember these basic rules:

- *Always phrase your affirmations in positive language.* Negative words send your unconscious boss a garbled message. For instance, you might think it would be effective to affirm: "I will never be afraid." But the word "afraid" conjures up feelings of fear even when you put a "not" in front of it. Remember that your boss is ruled more by emotions than by rational thought. Fear is such an overwhelming emotion that it blots out everything else in the message. Instead, affirm that you are *already* calm, strong, and steady.

- *Always use affirmations at alpha to reinforce your visualizations.* In this way you double the impact on your unconscious because you are using two senses rather than one to get your message across. Visualize that you are *already* acting with confidence and back up your mind picture with a *positive* affirmation.
- *Use affirmations at beta to reinforce positive thinking when you are feeling nervous.*
- *Use affirmations at alpha to prepare yourself for going into a situation that has caused anxiety in the past.*

Emotional Transfusion

Once you have mastered the art of simple visualizations and affirmations, you can go on to a very special technique for reprogramming your boss. This is a process I call Emotional Transfusion. To do it, you generate positive feelings in yourself by going into alpha and visualizing and affirming an experience that was wonderful. Then you transfuse these feelings into a second visualization—one in which you see yourself successfully accomplishing something that has caused you anxiety in the past.

Emotional Transfusion works like a blood transfusion. When your body is so weakened by disease or injury that no amount of medication can revive it, the doctor prescribes a transfusion of blood from a healthy donor. The additional white cells in the donor blood enable you to conquer the disease that is causing so much damage. By the same token, when you must participate in an activity that leaves you weakened with anxiety, you can use Emotional Transfusion to receive the healthy emotions that will fight off your tendency to feel afraid. Where do you get these healthy emotions? From yourself. You are both the donor and the receiver.

I first began using Emotional Transfusion when I realized that my unconscious was sending me feelings of inferiority whenever I tried to make a sales call. When I stood before a brand-new prospect, I stammered and apologized. I knew that I was making a bad impression, and the more I thought about how badly I was performing, the worse my presentation became. I also knew that the cure for this disease was to generate some confidence in myself so as to get over the panicky feelings. But my unconscious boss wouldn't let me, no matter how hard I tried.

To reprogram that boss, I first went into alpha and set up my *donor visualization*. This was the mental recreation of the time I almost made a hole in one while playing golf at the lovely course at Pebble Beach, California. I pictured myself on that beautiful green tee box while I listened to the waves lapping up against the rocks. I looked out to see the seals cavorting in the water. I smiled as I felt the sea breeze and the sun on my face. I saw myself hit the ball. Then, with a burst of elation, I watched it rise in the air, land on the green, and roll right up to the lip of the cup. I saw my whole face light up with exultation, pride, and self-confidence. I basked for a few moments in that wonderful glow that came from feeling more capable than I had ever felt in my whole life.

Next, with that mood of confidence pulsing through me, I quickly shifted from the donor visualization to the *receiver visualization*. I pictured myself talking to a new client. Since I didn't yet know what he looked like, I envisioned him as the very friendly stranger whom I had met one day in an art museum. I visualized my own face as it looked at the moment I saw the golf ball roll up to the edge of the Pebble Beach hole. I affirmed: "I am enjoying talking to my client as much as I enjoyed watching the ball almost roll into the cup at Pebble Beach.'' Then I pictured my client's face lighting up with excitement as though he had been there, too. In this way, I transfused the positive feelings of my donor visualization into my receiver visualization. I practiced this same Emotional Transfusion several days in my alpha sessions and again immediately before I made my actual call.

When I actually stood before my client, how surprised I was to find that my unconscious really did take over. The fear and anxiety I usually felt in such a situation evaporated. Although I didn't feel as relaxed as I would have had I actually been golfing with a friend, I was amazed to find that I *liked the client*. I felt interested in him as a person. I even enjoyed the challenge of selling him.

The strange and wonderful thing about Emotional Transfusion is that this tool not only allows you to stay calm in the face of a dreaded anxiety-producing activity, *it frees you to become more creative than a so-called "normal" person would be.* You are able to achieve even more because you become adept at clearing your mind of the negative thoughts that sap energy and undermine your resourcefulness. After I started using Emotional Transfusion frequently, my business improved by leaps and bounds.

I have used the Pebble Beach scene over and over as my donor visualization for facing all kinds of challenges. It has never failed. You, too, can lessen your feelings of anxiety and panic by simply visualizing an experience when you felt most competent and at ease as your donor visualization and then transfusing the feelings into your receiver visualization of an activity you have feared.

My Three-Day Program for Learning Emotional Transfusion

Day One: Go into alpha and play back some of your most enjoyable memories. You might remember the time you participated in a string quartet and heard the audience applauding your performance with gusto; the moment you saw your firstborn in the delivery room; the day your boss told your fellow employees how well you had performed; the sense of accomplishment you felt when you finished putting together your own television set using a kit and it worked; or the moment when the minister said, "I now pronounce you man and wife." Choose the experience that has the most emotion and feeling of accomplishment. Then visualize it in detail, including sounds, smells, expressions on the faces of yourself and others, and especially *your happy feelings*. Enjoy the glow.

Day Two: Select a situation that always causes you to feel anxiety. It might be an activity such as flying or being in a tunnel or crossing a bridge. Go into alpha and enjoy your donor visualization until you feel the glow of confidence and exhilaration. Immediately shift into a visualization of the situation that you fear—the airplane, the tunnel, or yourself in a car going over a bridge. Hold onto the look on your face in the donor visualization as you picture yourself in the receiver visualization. Affirm that you enjoy doing what you are doing just as much as you enjoyed the activity in the donor visualization.

Day Three: Think of a person with whom you have a poor relationship that causes you anxiety. This person could be someone with whom you work who always causes you to feel ill at ease or an unreasonable neighbor who seems to want to feud with you. Or it might be a family member with whom you have a poor relationship. Go into alpha and enjoy your donor visualization until you feel a glow. Then shift into your receiver visualization of the offending person and yourself. Picture the two of you engaged in a mutually enjoyable activity. Transfuse the good feelings from your donor visualization by picturing both your own and the other person's faces with the happy glow you experienced while doing the donor visualization. Affirm that you are feeling calm, happy, and exhilarated as you explain to that person that you enjoy being with him or her. See the other person feeling the same zest that you do. Then make an affirmation that you love that person.

I am not the only one for whom Emotional Transfusion has worked. Elizabeth was an extremely competent executive assistant to the chief executive officer of a large company. Unfortunately, the CEO reminded Elizabeth of her alcoholic father because he often blamed all his problems on her. He especially used her as a scapegoat when a board meeting was difficult. Lately Elizabeth had begun hyperventilating at work. She was at the point of giving up an excellent job when she discovered how to use Emotional Transfusion.

Elizabeth chose for her donor visualization the moment when she had been accepted as a member of her city's civic chorus. Elizabeth loved to sing and had a lovely voice, but she lacked formal training. She had never thought she was as good as the members of the civic chorus. When she auditioned and the director told her she was accepted, she felt extremely competent and elated.

Elizabeth practiced this donor visualization in alpha several times. When she had perfected it, she shifted to the receiver visualization. She pictured herself entering the CEO's office immediately after the board meeting. She visualized her boss with the same wonderful smile that he always had whenever he himself received an award. She saw her own face as radiant and happy as it was when the director invited her to become a member of the civic chorus. She affirmed, "I like talking to my boss about the problems that went on in the board meeting, because I am feeling as competent as I did the day I was selected for the civic chorus. I appreciate my talents."

Elizabeth didn't change her boss into a saint, but she did prevent herself from hyperventilating. Moreover, as she acted in a more confident manner, the CEO didn't use her as a scapegoat nearly so often.

Using the Second Basic Principle

Now that you have mastered the tools of visualization and affirmation, you can start using them to give yourself a self-image that will permit you to feel confidence rather than fear. Using the information about yourself that comes to you unbidden when you go to your secret resting place in alpha, you can reprogram yourself to become the person you want to be.

To recap, here are four rules for good visualizations and affirmations:

1. Make them positive.
2. Make them vivid and detailed.
3. Incorporate the emotions.
4. Use them frequently.

If you use visualizations and affirmations with the goal of overcoming anxiety for thirty days, you will see definite positive results. You will be able to work on desensitization more effectively, and you will be calm and relaxed.

CHAPTER 7

~~~~~~

How Not to Answer the Phone When Mr. Negative Calls: The Third Basic Principle

If you have used Emotional Transfusion to enable you to be calm under circumstances that previously generated anxiety, you know firsthand the power of the unconscious. Unfortunately, as you learned in Chapter 6, most of us also transfuse negative emotions to our unconscious through mind chatter and worry fantasies.

While I was having anxiety attacks, Mr. Negative ruled my life. I told myself that because I had anxiety, I was inferior to others and therefore unlovable. I couldn't achieve anything I set out to do. At the time I didn't know that these negative and irrational thoughts were filling my rain barrel with anxiety, causing my body to become so aroused that eventually it brought on the fight or flight response and helped the attacks perpetuate themselves.

Diabolically, each new panic attack caused me to think even more irrationally. It became a vicious cycle: negative thinking caused panic, which caused *more* negativity and hence more panic. As my phobia worsened, I told myself I was a total failure as a breadwinner and as a husband. I would never get any better. I was probably losing my mind. For six months, while I hid myself away in the house, I thought in those negative, irrational terms. Mr. Negative had me in his power.

Most of us don't realize that when Mr. Negative calls, we are reacting the same way we do when the telephone rings: we never think of *not* answering. We pick up the receiver, listen to the information that comes over the line, and then we act on it, even if we don't particularly like it. Of course, we have to answer the phone. It is ringing, isn't it?

The truth is, you don't have to answer! Once you recognize that irrational thoughts are devastating your life, you can *choose* not to answer Mr. Negative when he places his call. You can just let the phone ring and ring. If you don't pick it up, eventually Mr. Negative tires of making phone calls that are never answered. He gives up. By thinking rationally and positively about yourself, you can send good messages to your unconscious, which in turn will create a positive self-image for you.

My Third Basic Principle addresses two separate problems:

1. How to discern when you are thinking negatively and irrationally.
2. How to replace these distorted thoughts with positive, rational ones so that Mr. Negative will leave you alone.

Third Basic Principle: Use rational and positive thinking to see yourself and events as they really are and also to visualize how you want them to be.

By learning to think clearly without irrational distortions, you erase your negative self-image and become free to re-program yourself as you want yourself to be. I like to break this goal into what I call "The Five R's":

- *Realize* that Mr. Negative is part of your consciousness.
- *Recognize* when Mr. Negative is calling.
- *Refuse* to answer Mr. Negative.
- *Replace* negative and irrational thoughts with reality.
- *Relax* and reprogram the unconscious mind.

The First R: *Realize* That Mr. Negative Is Part of Your Consciousness

When we are prone to anxiety, many of us see the world as if we were looking at it through a fish-eye lens on a camera. We see all 360 degrees, but everything in view is distorted.

Some of us confuse the facts and fictions about ourselves because of our basic personalities. Maybe we are what some cardiologists call a Type A personality: we get our self-worth from working day and night. We never take time to relax. And we expect perfection of ourselves. If we don't achieve the pinnacle of success (and for Type A's, there's always another mountain peak behind the one they are climbing), then we are total failures.

Others may have a poor self-image because of having had unfortunate childhood experiences, handicaps, or an adult trauma. Still others see themselves in negative, irrational ways because they can't measure up to the unreasonable expectations someone else has put on them.

Once we discover that we are looking through the fish

eye, we can change lenses and see things as they really are. In fact, we can use an infrared filter and perceive things usually hidden by the dark.

People achieve extraordinary things when they choose the proper lens through which to view their limitations. Helen Keller was stricken with an illness that left her deaf and blind at the age of nineteen months. Yet she graduated from college with honors, wrote two books, toured the world, and promoted the education of persons similarly afflicted. Everywhere she went, she was revered for her extraordinary accomplishments. Jeff Blatnick won a gold medal at the 1984 Olympics in the Greco-Roman wrestling competition even though he learned two years previously that he had Hodgkin's disease. How did these two surmount such handicaps? *By focusing on the abilities they had rather than on their limitations,* they sent their unconscious a positive message. Their boss believed they could do great things and helped them achieve what the world calls a miracle.

The first step in overcoming a distorted view of ourselves is to realize that negative and irrational thoughts are a part of our consciousness. Once we admit the possibility that we are not thinking clearly, we can choose a new lens with which to look at ourselves, so that we can see our real potential.

The Second R: *Recognize* When Mr. Negative Is Calling

Being able to discern exactly when you are thinking negatively and irrationally is called *cognitive awareness*. The process of changing those thoughts into rational ones is called *cognitive restructuring*. This therapy, which has become an important part of the mainstream of modern psychiatric research and practice, holds that all moods are created by "cognitions," or thoughts. Your perception of what is happening to you—rather than the actual events themselves—affects the way you feel. And your mood determines your ability to function as you wish. For instance, when you're depressed or fearful, you open yourself to more anxiety, which undermines your ability to think, work, and relate well to people and situations.

Whenever you feel depressed, angry, or afraid, you can use cognitive restructuring to examine your thought processes and determine whether they are distorted. If you find you are not thinking clearly, you can replace the distortion with the reality of the situation. By adopting the rational thought patterns about what is going on in your life, you boost your mood and eliminate a certain amount of anxiety. In this way you can help yourself avoid panic attacks.

Scientific research under the critical scrutiny of the academic community has shown that cognitive restructuring is more effective in relieving depression than antidepressant drugs. And it is relatively simple to learn. You can do it either with a therapist or alone.

The Big Ten

Here is a list of the Big Ten cognitive distortions that affect most anxious people:

1. *Perfectionism* causes you to set unreasonably high standards for yourself and others. If you are a perfectionist, you may achieve at levels the world considers normal or even above par, yet see yourself as a failure or credit your accomplishments to mere luck. The reality of the situation is that you are a person of worth regardless of your achievements. You deserve love,

happiness, and self-acceptance as you are. You will have a lot less anxiety if you don't drive yourself to achieve unrealistic levels in everything you do.

2. *Rejectionitis* is the practice of exaggerating a single rejection until it affects everything else in your life. When your club elects your opponent as president, you believe your whole life is ruined. When a woman reacts coolly to you at a party, you tell yourself you're a social reject. Rejectionitis is like stuffing seemingly insignificant little grains of gunpowder into a cardboard cylinder. They're completely harmless unless you light them with a match. Then everything explodes.

   The reality of rejectionitis is that you cannot expect everyone else to prefer you to others. After all, you have your favorites among acquaintances, too. You do have qualities that appeal to some people. To prove that this is true, make a list of your good qualities and make another list of people who like you.

3. *Negative focus* is the habit of letting one negative situation in your life obliterate all the positives. It's looking through an electron microscope and seeing a cancer cell in all its horribleness without being able to see all the healthy cells around it. I used to use my leg as a negative focus. After I became an adult, no one ever said a word about my leg, but that didn't matter to me. Even if my leg was completely covered by my trousers, I thought that everyone else was aware of it and thinking about it whenever I became the center of attention. So I focused on it, too. As a result, I felt insecure and nervous. I sent more drops of stress to my rain barrel.

   The reality of this situation was that my leg was a big "so what?" to everyone but me. Besides, hardly anyone has a perfect body. People with far greater limitations than mine have achieved wonders. A good way to stop practicing negative focusing is to go to alpha and picture all the good things about yourself. Then affirm that they—and you—are great.

4. *Refusing the positives* goes a step farther than negative focus. You tell yourself that even the *good* things in your life are negatives! I used to do this when I told myself I was a business failure, even though I had an executive search firm of my own that had turned a profit by the time I was thirty. Why did I refuse to see that I was a success? My self-image was so poor and I was so overwhelmed by negative thoughts about myself that I couldn't feel comfortable thinking of myself as a success.

Most people who suffer from panic disorders are depressed. One form of refusing the positives and inviting depression is telling ourselves we can no longer do the things we used to enjoy. "I used to travel, go to the theater, play racquetball, and do book reviews for my club," you say. "But now those things bring on panic attacks." The reality is that your *attitude* brings on the attack, not the activity you once enjoyed.

You may go even farther with refusing the positives. If someone gives you a compliment, you turn it into a criticism. When your friend praises your hairdo, you reply, "Oh, it doesn't fit my lifestyle. I've got an appointment at the beauty parlor for a complete redo right now." Or if someone compliments your work, you immediately counter with "I was lucky to have clinched that deal. The competition backed out at the last minute." The reality is that most people don't pass out compliments if they don't want to give them. If they like something you did, rejoice! Let their image-building words nourish your unconscious.

Refusing the positives is a habit that's easy to end. When someone compliments you, just say, "Thanks," and *not another word*, no matter what you think. Eventually you will start believing the words are true.

5. The *white-is-black* phenomenon occurs when you use neutral or even positive facts to make negative conclusions. One of the most common ways to do this is to interpret someone else's actions as being hostile to you when they actually indicate that person's own discomfort. For instance, a clerk in a store snaps at you and you jump to the conclusion that you have done something wrong. In reality she is in a bad mood because she has just been taken to task by her boss.

I used to do white-is-black thinking when someone failed to return a business call to me. "I'm not important enough," I would tell myself. "Otherwise, he'd call back." I didn't stop to think that perhaps the caller was out of town or facing a business emergency or just plain too tired to make the call. I turned white into black and made myself feel inferior rather than looking at the situation as it really was and saving my self-esteem.

Another white-is-black kind of thinking takes place when you predict that everything you do will have dire consequences. I used to do that when I told myself I would have a panic attack and make a fool of myself if I went out in public. My white-is-black thinking brought on self-fulfilling trauma. I created enough anxiety about my panic disorder to make my aroused body generate adrenaline.

The way to "white out" the black is not with correction fluid but with reality thinking. Remind yourself that you are not the cause of everyone else's strange behavior. And recognize that you cannot know the outcome of a future event. Try predicting a happy ending instead of a tragedy for a change.

6. *Stretch-or-shrink thinking* is the habit of either stretching the truth into an anxiety-producing fiction when you've done something that you're less than proud of or of shrinking it until it's invisible if you did something good. When you stretch think, it's like blowing up one of those giant balloons used for parades. Deflated, the balloon is just a pile of limp plastic. Inflated, it becomes a dragon towering over you.

It's easy to stretch think when you make a simple mistake. Suppose you forgot your best friend's birthday. "She'll never forgive me. How could I have been so thoughtless? But that's just the way I am—a stupid, inconsiderate idiot," you tell yourself. The truth is that everyone forgets birthdays. A clue to how prevalent this mistake is is that the greeting card industry makes millions on belated birthday cards. Besides, if you were truly inconsiderate, you wouldn't be concerned. The reality is that you can apologize to your friend, celebrate her birthday after the fact, and the chances are you will be forgiven. If not, then your friend is the one who is distorting her thinking, not you.

By the same token, you may be shrinking all the good things about yourself until even you can't see them. When you do something that pleases you, take time to pat yourself on the back. Acknowledge yourself aloud, if you can. The reality is that you aren't being vain or conceited in complimenting yourself. You are sending good messages to your unconscious, which in turn will enable you to function without anxiety.

7. Creating *fictional fantasies* means letting your emotions substitute for the truth about what is happening. It's like feeling angry because today is the day you have to go to the dentist. "I got up on the wrong side of the bed," you tell your spouse. Because you *feel* angry, you act angry. You give yourself permission to nag as much as you like. When you think in fictional fantasies, you are apt to tell yourself that you are *feeling* anxious, and therefore you *are* anxious—too anxious to go to the supermarket. Or you are likely to wake up in the morning feeling sad because of a dream you can't remember. "I'm sad," you say, "and my life is a mess."

   Counter fictional fantasies by realizing that your distorted thoughts bring on negative feelings. Affirm that you are already feeling calm, happy, and at peace. Use Emotional Transfusion to change your feelings at the unconscious level.

8. *"Should" and "ought" legalisms* cause you to act in ways you would prefer not to simply because you believe some imaginary boss is telling you that you will be less than perfect if you don't. "I should make my bed, be on time, be nicer to my children," you tell yourself. Giving in to this tyrannous thinking can only lead to resentment and guilt. The reality is that you alone are responsible for your actions—not your father, mother, or the next-door neighbor. You are perfectly capable of setting up your own standards of behavior, and it really doesn't matter what others think about it. They are responsible only for their actions—not yours.

9. *Mistaken identity* means telling yourself you are all bad because you made a mistake. It's like putting on a dunce cap and wearing it forever because you broke a rule or because something bad, like an anxiety at-

tack, happened to you. "I'm just a dumb cluck," you say, putting on the dunce cap and sitting in the corner. "I'll never amount to anything." Or you didn't turn your body far enough around when you hit the tennis ball backhand, and you smashed it into the net. "I'll never learn," you moan.

The reality of mistaken identity is that everyone makes mistakes. You are still a person of worth even if you make one. You can make many positive contributions to life even if you fail dozens of times. Thomas Edison made thousands of mistakes before he invented a workable electric light bulb. Just try saying, "I made a mistake," and let it go at that.

10. Saying *"My fault"* assumes responsibility for a negative event even when the responsibility is not yours. In this case, *you* don't make the mistake. Others do. Yet you assume all the blame. If your husband drinks too much and makes a scene, you cry, "My fault," even though he was the one who tossed down six drinks in a row. Crying "My fault" inevitably builds up anxiety, because you can't make anyone else behave differently that way. The reality of "My fault" thinking is that no one can control another person, and no one should.

How Do *You* Think?

Did you recognize any cognitive distortions in your own thinking as you read this list? If not, perhaps the following quiz can help you discover ways in which you are causing yourself anxiety by not thinking clearly:

1. When you return from the supermarket, you check the

tape and discover that the clerk rang up ten dollars more than the actual cost of the groceries. Do you tell yourself you were stupid because you didn't catch the error at the check-out counter? If so, you are using *mistaken identity*. Sure, you made a mistake by not watching the cash register as the clerk checked each item. You may have been distracted or careless, but you aren't stupid. Everyone makes mistakes. You are still a person of worth who has doubtless made many intelligent decisions all day.

2. A person you'd like to have for a friend turns down your invitation to go to the theater because of a previous engagement. Do you tell yourself, "No one likes to do things with me. I'm just not much fun to be with"? If so, you are using *rejectionitis* thinking. The reality is that your prospective friend really may have had a previous engagement. And if not, one rejection doesn't mean that *no one* likes you. You can invite someone else. Or you can go alone and enjoy your solitude and autonomy.

3. Your boss tells you that you need to do further work on your last report because you missed some important data. Do you tell yourself, "I'm so inefficient, I'll never get a promotion"? This is a combination of *stretch-or-shrink* and *white-is-black thinking*. You are stretching the truth about your incomplete report and turning it into a dragon. At the same time, you are predicting dire consequences from the meeting with your boss. The reality is that by discussing the report with you, your boss is giving you a second chance to improve it. If you do well, he will likely be pleased. And you really have no way to tell whether you will ever get a promotion or not. Try thinking positively

and give your unconscious a chance to help you perform well enough to increase your chances.

4. Your best friend tells you you look lovely in the dress you're wearing. Do you answer, "This old thing? Why it's ten years old"? This is a clear-cut case of *refusing the positives*. Why not accept the compliment and enjoy the fact that you don't need the latest fashion fad to look smashing.

5. You meet your wife after work for a "Thank-God-it's-Friday" celebration, but your wife seems cool and refuses to laugh at your jokes. Do you tell yourself, "I must have done something wrong"? Unless she tells you you have done something wrong, you are likely doing "My fault" thinking. She may have had a hard time at the office. She may have a headache, or she may simply be tired.

6. You deliver a speech and leave out the main point you wanted to make. Do you berate yourself with "*I* was a total failure"? This is *perfectionism*. Maybe your speech wasn't letter-perfect, but that doesn't mean your audience didn't enjoy it. More than likely your listeners never realized you left out the main point. This could also be a case of *negative focus*—concentrating on one mistake and missing the bigger picture of success.

7. You sign a rental agreement for a new apartment. Do you tell yourself, "Since it's my apartment now, something is sure to go wrong with it"? This is *white-is-black* thinking—predicting dire consequences of your actions. You have no way of knowing whether something will go wrong with your apartment, and by predicting the worst, you are building up the anxiety level

in your rain barrel. Instead, savor the excitement of fixing up your new place.

8. You're feeling depressed for no reason you can figure out. Do you tell yourself, "The world is just no damn good"? If so, you are using *fictional fantasies*. You are letting your emotions substitute for the truth about what is happening. Yes, you are depressed, but the world is the same today as it was when you were feeling great. Try going into alpha and asking yourself why you are feeling depressed. Then use Emotional Transfusion to feel better about the situation that is causing your depression.

9. You refuse to contribute to the Fund for the Improvement of Living Conditions for Elderly Millionaires. Do you later punish yourself with the guilty thought, "I should have given at least ten dollars"? If so, you are subjecting yourself to *"should" and "ought" legalisms*. It's really okay to say no to anyone soliciting funds if you don't want to give. It doesn't matter what the elderly millionaires think about your keeping the ten dollars.

10. Your son flunks algebra. Do you tell yourself, "It's all my fault. I should have helped him more"? This is clearly *"My fault"* thinking. If your son doesn't study, he won't pass. You can't study for him. And crying "My fault" doesn't help you or him.

If you answered yes to any of these questions, you have been thinking irrationally. Either you didn't know that you were answering Mr. Negative's call, or you didn't know how to stop answering him—which is what you're going to learn next.

The Third R: *Refuse* to Answer Mr. Negative

It is one thing to recognize cognitive distortions after you have suffered the consequences. It is still another to be able to spot them while you are in the process of distorting so that you can immediately replace them with a positive thought. Here are some ways that I have learned to do this:

- Use the Blue Dot Technique to signal yourself when you are not thinking clearly. Previously I told you to paste blue dots in strategic places to remind yourself to relax. Now you can use the blue dots (or other colored dots if you wish to differentiate) for becoming aware of cognitive distortions. Each time your eyes falls on a dot, ask yourself what you are thinking about.

    When I did this, I pasted the blue stickers all around the house, my office, and even inside the car. I pasted one on my watch, so that every time I glanced at it I would remind myself to take stock of my thoughts. I was amazed at what I discovered about my mind chatter. I would be waiting at a traffic light when my eyes would fall on the blue dot I had stuck onto my dashboard. What was I thinking? "You stupid idiot, you'll never make your appointment in time. You should have left the office earlier!" I was shocked. Here I was *stretch-or-shrink* thinking. I was telling myself how stupid I was because I made the mistake of setting out late. Once I got to the appointment, I found that my unconscious had received my message literally. It obediently made sure that I acted stupid and stammered nervously when I made the call.

    Or, I would be waiting to meet the client in his office. I would glance at my watch and see the blue dot. Now what was I thinking? "Gee, look at the way this office is furnished. What gave me the idea that a little guy like me could win this contract?" This was *negative focus-*

ing. I was telling my unconscious I was "just a little guy" who wasn't too sharp, so of course I didn't deserve to get the contract.

When I became aware of such distorted thinking, I immediately affirmed that I was a person of worth, one who deserved success. Since I already had been affirming and visualizing these same things at the alpha level at home, I was able to stop these cognitive distortions at the feeling level—the level at which the unconscious more readily hears the message. That way they never even came close to the action level. I avoided creating situations that would have caused me problems.

- Use the Rubber Band Technique to reinforce reality thinking. Jim Wilson told me to wear a rubber band around my wrist. Whenever I discovered I was thinking negatively about myself, I was to snap this rubber band. The little jolt emphasized my return to reality. Like Pavlov's dog, I soon learned to react to this stimulus automatically. Just snapping the rubber band triggered positive thoughts.

- Cancel out your negative statements. A very quick, effective way to refuse to answer Mr. Negative's call is simply to tell yourself, "Cancel, cancel," every time you become aware that you are thinking or talking irrationally. This technique is effective when you are in the midst of a conversation and inadvertently hear yourself saying things like "Why did I do that? I sure am dumb!"

- Ask someone to help you pinpoint negative statements. When I asked Cindy to help me, I was amazed at how many times she caught me voicing negative thoughts. She pointed out that I was saying, "I just can't hit the ball without slicing it," and "Whenever I'm introduced to people, I just can't remember their names." And "I can't make a speech without getting the shakes."

If Cindy hadn't pointed out these "I can't" statements, I would never have realized I was saying them. I wouldn't have been able to cancel them out and quickly affirm, "I can." My unconscious would have kept on getting the message and obeying my "instructions" to make me fail.

In fact, I discovered you don't even have to say "I can't" to be negative. Listening to other people talking, I heard, "Whenever I have to wait in line, I get nervous." And "I am just worried sick about my husband." Without being aware of it, these people were sending the negative message "nervous" and "sick" to their unconscious. You can bet their boss went right to work to make them feel that way.

If you will ask others to help you spot the negative statements you have been making, you will become more conscious of the number of ways you and everybody else have been encouraging anxiety.

The Fourth R: *Replace* Negative and Irrational Thoughts with Reality

The Fourth R is *replacing* negative thoughts with positive ones to reprogram your unconscious. It involves planning ahead. You monitor your cognitive distortions and plan how you will confront them with reality. The easiest way to do this is to sit down with a pencil and a piece of paper that has three columns. The headings should be

1. Problem Thinking,
2. Cognitive Distortion, and
3. Positive Replacement.

106   ANXIETY AND PANIC ATTACKS

Find a quiet place where you can do some serious thinking about what has been happening in your life. To fill in the column headed "Problem Thinking," record thoughts that are creating negative emotions. These are thoughts that keep you from feeling good physically or prevent you from enjoying a happy relationship with a loved one or friend or interfere with your financial success, for instance.

Let's say you are angry because you invested a lot of time and effort in buying a new dress for your husband's annual company Christmas party. Your husband takes one look and says you are too heavy to wear such a youthful style. You smolder with rage. Your thoughts are that he's inconsiderate and unappreciative. At the same time you're telling yourself, "I'm ugly and inadequate and always will be. Nothing I do ever pleases him." Write down these thoughts about yourself in the first column.

In the second column, "Cognitive Distortion," write which one of ten cognitive distortions you are using to interpret the actual event. In this case, you would be using stretch-or-shrink thinking or fictional fantasies.

In the third column, labeled "Positive Replacement," write down the reality of the situation. You might write, "I am attractive because I have _____ ," and write down your good points. Or, write, "My husband does not like the new dress, but it is not necessary for him to approve of everything I wear. I like the way I look in this dress. I enjoy wearing it."

Here are some other examples of how you can replace irrational thoughts with reality. A rational response to "I have a knot in my stomach that keeps me from giving a speech; everybody will notice my nervousness" is "Everybody's nervous giving a speech. It's quite all right to experience that feeling. I am very capable of speaking." An irrational "Nobody loves me" can be replaced with "I can think of three or four people who love me." And the thought "I can't love myself because I've made so many mistakes" can be replaced with "Everybody makes mistakes. I can forgive myself just as I would another who did the same thing. Besides, I have many lovable qualities."

The actual process of writing down these positive statements on paper is a way of communicating with your unconscious. You are letting your unconscious boss know firmly that you are not going to accept his irrational feelings. Once you get the hang of writing down negative thoughts and replacing them, you will have discovered how not to answer Mr. Negative when he calls.

The Fifth R: *Relax* and Reprogram the Unconscious Mind

With the Fifth R, you can learn to reprogram your unconscious so that you never even hear Mr. Negative ringing. You do this by relaxing—going into alpha and using the carefully planned visualizations and affirmations you learned to formulate in Chapter 6.

While I was having panic attacks, I often had the irrational thought that if I went outside the house another panic attack would hit me. Either I would die from a heart attack or I would lose control of myself and run through the streets ripping off my clothes and shouting terrible obscenities. I could tell myself as many times as I wished that these symptoms were simply my body's fight or flight response to anxiety and that I wouldn't die, but I still had strong fears. Every time I pictured myself having a panic attack or chattered to myself with worry, I delivered a strong message to my unconscious to bring on more anxiety.

To counteract my white-is-black thinking, I confronted myself with reality. "Physiologically, I am perfectly normal. I now know how to deal with anxiety," I told myself.

Then I would go into alpha and reprogram my unconscious with these affirmations: "Whenever I go outside, my body is perfectly relaxed. I enjoy going outside." I would visualize myself going wherever I wanted, a smile on my face as I did interesting things.

After confronting my distorted thinking and reprogramming positive thoughts at alpha several times a day, my unconscious began to believe I was already going many places and feeling fine. Then when I actually did venture forth, my unconscious sent me good feelings rather than anxious ones. Mr. Negative never even managed to make the phone ring!

You can use the Fifth R, Relax and Reprogram, to think clearly about any problem. Perhaps you tell yourself, "I am just plain unattractive because I'm too short . . . too tall . . . too thin . . . too fat." Write down your distorted thinking. Then make a list of all the realities that apply to you. List ten attractive things about yourself. Maybe you have a good complexion, even teeth, luxuriant hair, nice cheekbones, a lovable personality, and sympathy for others. Come on, everyone has ten good appearance and personality characteristics. List them, then spend some time relaxing at alpha. Picture and affirm your good points and you will be surprised at how much more attractive you feel when you are around those whom you want to impress. Why? Your unconscious will send you the good feelings that allow you to be charming and relaxed around others. You can't help but seem more attractive.

Briefly, here are the steps to follow to prevent Mr. Negative from calling:

1. Write down your distorted thinking.
2. Confront your distortions with reality.
3. Write down ten positive ways in which the reality applies to you.

4. Go into alpha and visualize and affirm that these realities are already true for you.
5. Relax and let your unconscious recreate your self-image.

Manufacture the Positive

Now that you have seen how cognitive distortions increase anxiety, you know that thoughts are like mood-creating products which you manufacture in your brain. You can generate good, positive thoughts that will build you up and keep you calm, or you can let bad thoughts roam around in your mind, creating anxiety and a bad self-image.

You need to remember that you are the plant manager! You can *choose* which thoughts you want to manufacture. Realizing I had that choice was a real awakening for me. I didn't have to let my negative thoughts manipulate my life! By confronting my cognitive distortions with reality, then programming myself to think positively, I could prevent Mr. Negative from getting through to me.

CHAPTER 8

~~~~~~

How Not to Play the Role of Victim: The Fourth Basic Principle

One day I received a phone call from a man I'll call Jerry who seemed embarrassed to tell me that he had a problem. He had been trying to prepare himself for a new career by attending a real estate course. But sitting in class made him so nervous he couldn't concentrate. Finally he told the teacher he was going to have to drop out. Since she was a friend of mine, she told him to call me.

"I understand that you had a similar condition and that you got over it," he began. "But I doubt you can help me. I've been this way for five years. Every time I go out of the house, I feel nervous. I can barely keep from crying. I get so embarrassed I can't stand it. Why did this have to happen to me?"

It was apparent that Jerry saw himself as a victim of circumstances, doomed to stay at home for the rest of his life. I assured him I knew exactly how he felt. I used to feel like a victim, too.

"Yet there is a way you can get over your anxiety symptoms," I told him. "It's an easy way, too, but you have to take the responsibility for doing something about it."

"I'll do anything," Jerry said. "Tell me what to do."
First, I told him, he would do well to see a psychologist and get some insight into why his rain barrel was so full of anxiety. Next, he needed to learn how to use the tools of visualization and affirmation to fool his unconscious boss into believing he was already calm and happy. Then he needed to reinforce this message to his unconscious by *acting as if* he were already calm and relaxed outside the home.

Jerry took my advice. After a few weeks he was so excited about his progress that he phoned and told me he had written out what he called a "Declaration of Personal Responsibility." Here's what he wrote:

I currently possess the ability to be calm, relaxed, and at ease with other people. I have a normal body and a normal mind. When my rain barrel overflows with so much anxiety that my body brings on a fight or flight response, it is because I have not used the mental tools of visualizing, affirming, and thinking clearly. I now take full responsibility for using all these tools to reprogram my mind.

While my body is not yet as free of anxiety symptoms as I want it to be, I recognize that I have a choice: I can act *as if* I am the way I want to be and thus reinforce my mental programming. Or I can refuse to act that way and remain anxious and afraid. I now resolve that I will take the initiative and act the way I need to in order to make myself calm and at peace.

I complimented Jerry on his change of attitude. No longer was he willing to play the role of victim.

"How exactly are you going to act out this resolution?" I asked.

"I'm going to do a lot of things differently," he told me. He had learned through cognitive awareness that he was a Type A personality, so he was going to stop expecting perfection of himself. He was going to work at desensitizing himself from his fears of being in crowds and not blame himself if he didn't become symptom-free in a single day. Furthermore, he was going to set aside at least one afternoon a week when he could do whatever he liked without feeling guilty. He was going to join a spa and get some exercise every day so that he could relax. And at work he was going to adopt a whole new way of functioning. No longer was he going to try to do two things at once, such as writing a memo while waiting on "hold" on the telephone. He also was going to delegate some responsibilities rather than doing everything himself.

It was apparent that Jerry was practicing my Fourth Basic Principle in everything he did:

Fourth Basic Principle: Act as if you are already the way you want to be.

Acting *as if* is living as you *intend* to live. It is creating a game plan for changing the destructive behaviors that cause you anxiety and then taking responsibility for living *as if* the game plan is already fulfilled. If you are depressed, it could mean reading a joke book to find funny stories you can tell others—even when you don't find the jokes amusing yourself. Why? Because you know that by acting *as if* you are happy, you are training your unconscious to stop being depressed. You are no longer allowing yourself to be the victim of fictional fantasy thinking.

When you visualize and affirm that you are calm, you are fooling your unconscious into believing that you are already that way. Acting *as if* is the hammer that nails the positive message in so firmly that it sticks for good.

How Acting *As If* Works

How can living as you intend to live cause your brain to stop activating the glands that secrete the corticosteroids that bring on a panic attack? Think of your brain as if it were a muscle that becomes skilled through endless repetition. When you first sit down at the piano, your fingers, directed by the part of your brain responsible for motor actions, are stiff and clumsy. It is all you can do to play "Mary Had a Little Lamb" with the fingers of one hand. But you keep on practicing. After weeks of scales and finger exercises, you progress to chords, two hands, and "Moonlight Sonata." If you keep on acting out your intention to play the piano, your fingers eventually learn to move as you want them to without your thinking of each individual motion. But of course it is not your fingers that play jazz innovations on their own. They are controlled by your brain. And your brain has learned this new skill because you first intended to do it and then practiced exercises daily to reinforce and expand your new skills.

If you diagram the process of learning to play the piano it looks like this:

Intention ⟶ Exercises (acting out) ⟶
Change in brain ⟶ Motor skill

The same dynamics bring on panic attacks. Let's suppose you are in the habit of thinking negatively or telling yourself you are depressed, nervous, or unable to go outside. Or you tell yourself other people don't like you. Although you certainly don't *want* a panic attack, you don't commit yourself to an active program that will help you avoid it. Your brain translates your ignorance of how to overcome panic as a lack of intention. The message that you're depressed or unable to go outside comes across loud and clear to your unconscious, which sets about making sure that you really do feel nervous and depressed. Then you reinforce these negative emotions by telling other people all your troubles or sitting in the house hiding away from everyone. Your actions cause your rain barrel to overflow. Diagrammed, this negative learning process would look like this:

Lack of intention——→Negative acting out——→
Reinforcement of negative thought processes——→
Continued panic attacks

On the other hand, you can do your scales every day—go into alpha and affirm and visualize a happier you. Then you act *as if* you are happy with other people and reinforce your brain's ability to think positively. Soon you are making beautiful music without being aware of how you do it. You are going wherever you want and feeling perfectly relaxed. Here's the way this positive learning process is diagrammed:

Intention (visualizing and affirming)——→Positive reinforcement (acting as if)——→Changed brain response——→Calm feelings

By intending and acting out, we cause *actual changes* to take place in the physical brain. Simply stated, a normal human nervous system consists of the brain and spinal cord and their nerves. Stimuli from the environment prompt sensory nerves to deliver impulses to the spinal cord; motor nerves direct them from the cord to the muscles and glands. The research of Sir John Eccles, who won the Nobel Prize in 1963 for the discovery of the chemical means by which impulses are communicated or repressed by nerve cells, bears this out. He has proven that the supplementary motor area of the brain contains what can be regarded as the "inventory" of all the learned motor programs of the brain and their "addresses" in the brain. Your intention to perform some action uses this inventory as if it were a great card index system to activate the learned motor programs and so bring about the desired or willed movement. By acting out your new intention, you create a new motor program—a new address called "Calm Street"—in your brain.

The Two Laws of Learning

When you act *as if*, you are using two well-known psychological laws governing learning. *The law of association* was first described by Aristotle when he recognized that human beings who were presented with a given stimulus or general situation could make a new response that was different from their traditional behavior. In the twentieth century, Ivan Pavlov used the laws of association to formulate his famous experiment on the conditioned reflex. He rang a bell whenever he presented meat to a dog. Eventually he took away the meat, rang the bell, and found that the dog still responded by salivating. The animal had learned to associate the bell with his food. His body, in turn, made the conditioned response of salivating. When you act *as if*, you are using the laws of association to cause your body to respond in a new and calm way.

Acting *as if* also employs the method of learning that psychologists call *operant conditioning*. Researchers have taught cats the steps to opening a cage in which they were locked by giving them a reward of food when their random movements were the proper ones. When behavioral therapists want to help patients overcome negative habits, they use operant conditioning by reinforcing the desired response with praise or some other reward. When you act *as if*, you are using operant conditioning on yourself. Your reward comes in the form of encouragement from others when they see you acting more positively, as well as a feeling of accomplishment within yourself.

Acting *as if* is a clear message to the brain that you intend to be calm, happy, and composed. Your brain in turn searches its card index system and sends the message to your glands not to rush adrenaline into the bloodstream. Through your intentions and your actions, your brain is programmed with a new response to a stimulus that in the past made you anxious.

How to Act *As If*

When you first start acting *as if*, you may feel strange. You may be affirming to yourself, "I am perfectly calm and relaxed when I go to the shopping mall." But when you actually face the people, the long halls, and the confusion of noise, smells, and lights, your heart may begin to beat harder. Your unconscious says, "Oh, no, *you're* not going to be calm. You're going to have a panic attack right here." By going ahead and acting as calm as you can, you demonstrate your intention to your brain. You are setting up a new association about shopping malls: you feel perfectly calm there and that's that. Just as you can "fool" your unconscious with visualizations and affirmations, you also fool it by acting *as if*. When you persist despite discomfort, your unconscious eventually receives the message and begins to send you positive feelings about making trips to malls.

Willard Scott, the weatherman on a national TV show and a board member of the Phobia Society of America, frequently feels anxiety symptoms before the cameras turn on him. Scott got professional help for his phobia and developed ways that helped him appear to be calm while on the air. I believe that through his acting *as if* he was perfectly calm while on the air, he trained his unconscious to respond differently.

You can use acting *as if* for more than desensitization, however. After I looked at the cognitive distortions that were causing my poor self-image, I decided to use acting *as if* to reinforce the reprogramming I was doing at alpha to change my twisted thinking. Before I made this resolution, I used to tell everyone I met how grim the day was. I reported every twinge I felt to anyone who would listen. When I began practicing acting *as if*, I started telling everyone, "I feel great. It's a wonderful day." And I did begin to feel better.

When I found myself getting impatient with my mother, my wife, or a business associate, I not only affirmed to myself that I was a calm, loving person, I acted *as if* by responding to them in a pleasant tone of voice and discussing differences rationally. Even though I was boiling inside, I recognized that by acting *as if* I were calm, I was training my sensory nerves to deliver different messages to my spinal cord, which in turn sent a different message to my brain. Like bad-tasting medicine, these difficult actions were going to make me well.

How to Make the Medicine Go Down

Perhaps you are saying, "It's impossible for me to react calmly to something that makes me mad." Let me assure you that I could do that only after visualizing and affirming myself as calm in regular alpha practice sessions before the disagreement took place. When I used the reprogramming techniques and reinforced them along with acting *as if*, my emotions began to change. I really was calm. My anxiety decreased.

Operant conditioning also played its part. I patted myself on the back each time I responded to an irritating situation with self-composure. I felt better about myself, and with a better self-image I was no longer overly sensitive.

What I am saying may sound like the exact opposite of the advice of psychologists who urge you to admit your true feelings. "Go ahead, get angry, punch your pillow, yell, scream," we read in their books. I am not saying you will never feel angry at something someone does and that you must not ever express this, or that the death of a loved one or a tragic accident will not cause you to be depressed. What I am saying is that it is counterproductive to reinforce the idea that you are a *victim* of circumstances, with *no choice* about how to feel or how and when to express your emotions.

"Look at what she did to me," you cry when you play the role of victim. You rant on for half an hour about how "she" took advantage of you. All you are doing in this case is sending emotional messages to your unconscious, which in turn causes you to remain angry, helpless, and subject to anxiety. How much better to say, "I am very angry at this woman, and I know this anger can cause me to feel anxiety. I need to find ways to be calm." In this case, you are sending your unconscious the message that despite your anger, your intention is to be calm. You will take the responsibility for becoming that way.

By all means, seek out a therapist or close friend and share your deepest feelings if they are causing you problems. But express your feelings in a way that acts out your determination to feel the way you want to. Then go out and act *as if* to reinforce the message.

A prominent politician who had a fear of flying wanted to be governor of his large state. But he knew that he could never cover the territory by auto, so he resolved to get over his phobia. He worked on desensitizing himself by first going to the airport, then going inside a plane, and finally taking a short flight. When the election campaign began, he still had qualms about flying, but he acted *as if* he were perfectly composed. He won the election and since has flown all over the world. I am convinced that his determination to act *as if* helped him win the election and have an outstanding career.

Tips for Acting *As If*

Everyone's game plan for acting *as if* is different, since all of us have different situations that cause us anxiety. Here are some general ways that will make it easier for you to practice acting *as if* regardless of your own particular anxiety-producing stressors:

- Quit listening to radio newscasts and reading newspapers while you are learning to practice *as if*. I found it was easier for me to think positively and to act *as if* I felt that life was great if I didn't hear or read about a lot of catastrophes, high taxes, inflation, crime, and dishonesty. Just listening to bad news was enough to put me in a gloomy mood.

For the period while I was desensitizing myself and trying to act in positive ways, I just wasn't strong enough to listen to all that misery and say, "I feel wonderful."

• Avoid being with people who are negative. When you are listening to others playing the "Ain't it awful" game, it's a temptation to top their troubles with one of your own. Before you know it, you've delivered a dramatic monologue titled "Poor me." That kind of talk goes straight to your unconscious and causes you to see yourself as a victim who can't do anything to stop anxiety.

• Read inspirational or positive-thinking books the first fifteen minutes of your day. Blot out negative thoughts before they have a chance to begin.

• Join the Phobia Society of America, 133 Rollins Avenue, Suite 4B, Rockville, MD 20852 (301) 231-9350. This is a nationwide group of therapists, doctors, and recovering phobics who not only sponsor informative regional programs about panic disorders, but can also function as a support group that will help you learn and practice techniques for dealing with your panic and anxiety. Members well know how effective desensitization is because they have experienced it firsthand. Furthermore, they do not reinforce the idea that once you have become subject to anxiety you will always be that way. Instead, they give you positive feedback. They make operant conditioning work for you.

• Give yourself lots of "attaboys!" I know one man in the Phobia Society who uses a calendar to record an "attaboy!" for each day. These are ways that he has successfully acted *as if*. For instance, on Day One, he might write: "Spent 15 minutes in the library." On Day Two, he might record,

"Spent 20 minutes in the library." On Day Three, he might write, "Stayed calm at J's," and on Day Four, "Cut back one tranquilizer pill." You get the idea. Each day when he wrote down his "attaboy!" he gave himself positive feedback. He saved each month's sheets and frequently went back and read his "attaboys!" to remind himself how far he'd come.

- Before attempting to act *as if*, always program at alpha. Jim Wacker, football coach at Texas Christian University, made headlines by using visualizations and affirmations with his team before they acted out their plays in a game. In 1983, this Fort Worth–based university won only a single game the entire season. During the 1984 training period, Wacker taught his players how to visualize themselves as performing with flawless technique. He encouraged the team to act *as if* they were as proficient as their mental imagery. During the 1984 season, football fans from across the nation were awed by the TCU performance. This team finished the season with eight wins and three losses and received its first invitation to play in a bowl game since 1959. Wacker himself was selected as national coach of the year by several sports organizations.

Why Most People Don't Act *As If*

In working with others, I've learned there are three reasons why people don't get over their anxiety:

- Fear of change,

- Belief that they can't break a bad habit, and
- Ignorance of how to go about it.

Fear stems from the strange thought that we will be different from the way we were in the past. What will other people think? No matter how unproductive our way of living has been, we at least know what it's like living with anxiety. We don't know what it is like to remain calm around others or to stop requiring perfection of ourselves. So we're afraid.

Take it from one who has felt just that way. A new, calmer lifestyle is well worth the slight discomfort you may feel as you act *as if*. Once others recover from the shock of seeing the new you, they will tell you how happy they are for you. In my case, my desire to overcome panic attacks outweighed my fear of change. I began to make a game of acting *as if*. I began to conjure up some good feelings. Then my body began to respond. The rain barrel level went down. At the first level, I stopped having panic attacks. At the next level, I stopped having anxiety feelings. Finally, the rain barrel was completely drained. My fear of panic attacks was gone, and so was my fear of change.

As for bad habits, you may think you are too old to change if you have been seeing yourself as a victim for twenty or thirty years. You're not. I know people in their seventies and eighties who have broken habits through using the unconscious and acting *as if*. Being anxious is just a habit, and you can break habits.

Although it may be true that nobody ever gave you an "owner's manual" that told you how to change, you now know that practicing my Five Basic Principles is an effective way to remain calm. It doesn't matter that the school you attended, like mine, never said a word about how your mind operated. Now that you know the way to change, all you have to do is take responsibility for doing the step-by-step actions that will enable you to change. It's like planting a garden. Digging the soil, applying fertilizer, and then weeding require an investment in time and actions. But once all that is done, you can sit back and enjoy your luscious yield.

CHAPTER 9

~~~~~~

How to Draw Your Own Treasure Map: The Fifth Basic Principle

One day my friend Tom called and asked me to have lunch with him. No sooner had the waiter taken our order than he heaved a big sigh.

"Boy, I'm bushed. I didn't sleep a wink last night. I feel terrible. In fact, the reason I called you is that something's drastically wrong with me. I feel like I'm about to crack up," he said.

Tom was one of those fellows who appeared to have everything. I'd watched him climb to an executive position with his company by the time he was thirty-eight. He, his wife, Jane, and their two children lived in a prestigious neighborhood. Tom flew his own plane. They traveled. Their kids swam in their own backyard pool.

"What's wrong, Tom?" I asked. For months now I had noticed Tom's chain smoking, his frantic busyness. Now I saw that his hands shook when he picked up his glass.

"Nothing, really," he said, then gave a wry smile. "I mean everything. We've got a bunch of problems at the office. And at home I've got two teenagers. Need I say more?"

"I don't understand," I said. Then he told me his kids were running around with a bunch of losers that he was sure were drug abusers. When he tried to make his son and daughter come in by midnight, they didn't pay any attention. The more he punished them, the less they studied. He was sure both were flunking. Whenever he tried to have a serious talk with them, they told him he was old-fashioned.

The more Tom talked, the more it sounded as if he were the unwilling victim of circumstances.

"I stay at work as long as I can. When I do finally have to go home, I fortify myself with two or three Scotch and waters," he told me.

By contrast, Tom found it a pleasure to serve his annual two-week tour of duty as an officer in the army reserve.

"Everything works like it's supposed to there. I give orders and those below me follow them. But at home, I've just lost control. And Jane isn't much help, either," he said.

When I visited Tom's home one weekend, the air of hostility was so thick I could almost smell the gunpowder. Tom wasn't communicating with his family. He was ordering them around like soldiers under fire. And he was right: nobody did what he ordered.

Furthermore, Tom and Jane played a constant game of one-upmanship. He kept telling her the children's bad manners were all her fault. She let him know she was a victim of circumstances, too. What could she do about it when she always had a headache or a nervous stomach or an aching back?

Time for a Detour

It was obvious to me that Tom needed to make a change in his lifestyle. He needed to set goals for better relationships with his wife and children and for a better physical condition. Then he needed to act out these goals by learning how to stop trying to control everything his wife and children did. He needed to learn communication skills. And he should avoid the cigarettes and alcohol that were taking such a toll on his body. He needed to eat right and take time from his work for some golf or tennis or whatever was recreation for him.

"There's a better way to deal with all your anxiety," I told him. "You don't have to live like this." But when I mentioned some of the changes in lifestyle that would help, Tom just shook his head.

"Bob, I'm too old to change now. Besides, my situation is really no different from my friends'. I see documentaries on television all the time about teenagers who act just like my kids."

Then he proved he was a victim with this final argument: "That's just the way life is."

Poor Tom. Try as I might, I couldn't convince him that he didn't have to live in all that misery. Perhaps he couldn't change the problems at work or his wife or children. But he could stop playing the victim and change himself! He could set goals that would help him carry out his intentions to change, then use my Five Basic Principles to make the changes easier. By so doing, he could prevent his anxiety level from reaching the spillover point in his rain barrel. He could avoid a full-fledged panic attack simply by making a detour in the path he was following.

My Fifth Basic Principle

In Chapter 8 you learned that the first step in making the changes in your brain to prevent anxiety and panic attacks was to *intend* to change. The next step was to act *as if* you had already changed. And you could make acting *as if* easier by reprogramming your unconscious through visualizations and affirmations. If you did all this, your brain would not send messages to your glands to emit panic-causing corticosteroids.

My Fifth Basic Principle gives you a concrete way to carry out these good intentions:

Fifth Basic Principle: Set goals to become the person you want to be.

"Is that all?" you may ask. "Goal setting is old hat. I've tried that." But have you ever set goals for the specific purpose of overcoming anxiety? Have you ever coupled goal-setting with the other techniques for using the unconscious which will make goal-achieving easy?

A lot of people, like Tom, know that they have a problem. They don't like the poor relationships, the stressful job, the unpleasant physical symptoms. Their secret hope is that a bolt of lightning will wipe out their misery in one crackling instant. But wishing and hoping don't bring about change. Goals do. Goals outline the steps you can follow one day at a time to make change possible. Like treasure maps, they show the way to riches so wonderful you can't even imagine them. They reassure you that if you follow the path, you will arrive at the destination you want.

I used to wait for a bolt of lightning to reduce all my problems to ashes, too. I wished that I did not feel inferior to my friends. I wished I was as capable as my fellow workers. I longed for others not to reject me. More than anything in the world, I wanted not to feel so bad about myself. I had a whole boxcar of wishes and wants, but no goals toward which my train could travel. Therefore, I didn't move one inch closer to fulfilling those wishes.

I now realize that the wishes and wants I had were based on deep negative feelings that only sent a message to my unconscious to make me feel more inferior. "I sure wish I wouldn't have another panic attack when I go outside," I would tell myself, all the while worrying and picturing the dire results. My unconscious responded to this message by increasing my anxiety, so that I actually had more panic attacks. Like it or not, wishes can become goals for your unconscious to carry out. And often the wishes are phrased in a negative manner.

I first considered replacing wishes with goals while I was reading books about the importance of having a good self-image. While I was in alpha at my secret resting place, I began to ask myself what choices I had about changing my life. The answer came back: I could continue to wish I were different, or I could commit myself to setting goals and acting out the changes I needed to make to achieve them. I promised myself I *would* set goals. I *would* achieve what I wanted.

I don't mind saying that I consider this chapter on goals the most important one in this book. You can learn all the techniques about programming your mind with visualizations and affirmations that you want. You can study rational thinking till you're an expert. *But if you don't take charge and commit yourself to action, you are just daydreaming!* You must set goals and set them correctly, and then act on them, or all the rest won't do a thing for you.

Getting Started with Goals

Before you sit down with a piece of paper to write down your goals, look at some of the criteria for succeeding in achieving them.

1. You must have a *burning desire* to succeed in the goal. Your goal should be so *important* to you, it should be so *big,* that it will make you excited enough to practice visualizing, affirming, and acting *as if.* If your goal is only to feel better tomorrow than you felt today, that's not much to motivate you. If your goal is to feel better tomorrow than you've *ever felt in your life,* you'll turn on that surge of electricity, that flow of adrenaline, that will empower you to do what you need to do. Yes, your boss will do all the work, but not unless you carry out your intention to act *as if.*

   My first big goal was to become a happy, confident, loving, and caring person. Just thinking that I could become the kind of man I had always envied excited me. Could I really do it? Yes, because I had found the road map I needed. I knew I could set my goal, reach my unconscious boss, and let him help me act *as if.*

2. Your goal must be *believable.* Your subconscious may balk if your goal is to transform yourself instantly from fat to slim. But if you select a *long-term* goal of losing weight, your unconscious will believe you can do it and will work to help you achieve it.

   Facing the complete transformation needed to reach some goals is mind-boggling unless you take them one step at a time. The solution is to break most goals into increments of daily and sometimes even hourly goals. The smaller the increment, the better. Let's say your goal is to lose fifty pounds. That seems like an awesome amount. Even though you're excited about the prospects of fitting into a size eight dress, it is hard to believe that you really can do it. But if you make your goal to lose fifty pounds over the period of a year, you can break it down into increments as small as one pound a week. That doesn't seem like so much. You can do it!

Breaking your long-term goal into increments allows you to reap the benefits of *operant conditioning*. The feeling of accomplishment you gain from losing one pound is encouragement to maintain your diet and exercise.

When I set the goal of improving my golf game, I automatically received feedback every thirty days. My club posted each member's handicaps at the beginning of each month, so I could actually see my handicap decreasing. Everyone else could, too. I felt encouraged to continue to program myself to achieve my goal. This "attaboy!" was like adding another log onto the fire of my burning desire.

Choosing Positive Phrasing for Your Goals

3. Make your goals *positive,* not negative. Write down what you *want*, not what you don't want. In other words, avoid writing, "I don't want to be fat anymore," or "I don't want to feel nervous," or "I don't want to fuss at my children." Instead, write, "I see myself thin," "I see myself calm," or "I see myself loving my children and being patient and understanding."

After I learned to make positive rather than negative goals, my golf technique improved. The course I played on had one hole with a water hazard. I used to repeat the goal I had made, "I will not hit the ball in the water," right before I teed off. My unconscious must have heard only "hit the ball in the water," because invariably that's what I did. Later I made a positive goal: "On hole number 15, I will hit the green on the first stroke." I spent time at alpha picturing the ball hitting the green and rolling into the hole. I avoided picturing the water at all. Then my ball started almost miraculously staying dry.

4. Set goals in all areas of your life. To become calm under all circumstances, you must include goals for your mental, physical, and spiritual well-being. If you don't, your unconscious will likely fill the void with whatever thoughts are left running around unleashed. For most of us, those thoughts are negative. Many anxious people get hung up by setting goals only on their health, careers, and finances. They forget you cannot be the calm, secure person you want to be unless you take a holistic view of yourself.

Your Goal Book

Here's how to plan your own goals. Buy yourself a looseleaf notebook that is small enough to fit in your pocket or handbag so that you will have it with you every time an idea pops into your head. But be sure it can expand to hold thousands of goals. The more goals you have, the more you will achieve.

Divide your notebook into three areas—"Mental," "Physical," and "Spiritual." You may want to subdivide these areas with further headings. Under "Mental," you could have a subdivision for "Habits to Break" heading a list of goals for giving up tranquilizers, stopping smoking, or drinking less. You could have another subdivision labeled "Family Relationships" with a separate goal sheet for each person in your family. Under "Physical," you might have a subdivision titled "Health," which could include goals for losing weight, practicing fitness routines, or overcoming a specific illness. Under "Spiritual," you might place a subdivision titled "Learning about Spiritual Practices" with goals for reading certain books. It is important to have goals in all three of the main areas.

To begin setting goals, first go into alpha and while you are at your secret resting place, ask yourself what the burning desires are in your life. Most of us do have bonfire-sized desires. We may long to become more relaxed, to be able to leave our houses, and to face the world without anxiety. But we may also long to find the perfect spouse or improve our health or excel in racquetball. These burning desires should become your goals.

If you feel you have no burning desires, just continue to go to alpha and let your unconscious speak to you. Be patient. You will come up with some ideas. Don't evaluate them, just let them surface. All you need to get started is one goal. By writing it down, you will enhance your contact with your unconscious. Soon your boss will be sending you unexpected messages about goals you didn't realize you wanted. You will "hear" about these goals while you are meditating, after you've gone to bed, when you first wake up, or even during busy periods of the day. That's why it is wise to carry your goal book with you wherever you are. If you don't write down these ideas immediately, you are likely to forget them.

Of course, you won't be able to work on all these goals at once, but it's important to have them. Once you know you have a road map in hand, you can stop worrying that you'll never find the way to that particular treasure. It is also a promise that further treasures are in store.

On the Road

After identifying your burning desires in the areas of mental, physical, and spiritual well-being, select the one you consider the most important. Write this goal on a separate sheet of paper along with all the directions you will need to reach the treasure. Here is what you should record:

1. The goal, stated in a positive manner.
2. Specific visualizations and affirmations of yourself as if you had already achieved that goal.
3. The cognitive restructuring you believe is necessary to help you achieve the goal.
4. The increments of the goal that reflect how you will act *as if* you have already reached the goal.

How do you know which goal to work on first? Your unconscious will prioritize your needs if you let it. If you have agoraphobia, you may want to set an initial goal of simply being able to leave the house. If your anxiety isn't that extreme, but you are in terrible physical condition, then your first priority could be physical fitness.

My first inclination was to work on my goal of ridding myself of phobic symptoms. But when I listened to my unconscious, it told me that it was more important to be able to feel better about myself. In fact, I would recommend to anyone who is having anxiety attacks to work first on that goal. Why? If you can build your self-esteem by becoming confident, loving, and caring, you will not have anxiety attacks.

If I hadn't first learned to feel better about myself, my unconscious would have interfered every time I tried to think positively about accomplishing some of the things I needed to do to eliminate anxiety. If I had tried to remain calm in the face of criticism or to make a better sales presentation while I had a poor self-image, my negative unconscious would have said, "Oh, no! You can't do that. You're just not that kind of person!"

Here's what I wrote on my goal sheet. I stated my goal as "I see myself as a loving, self-confident person." Under visualizations, I stated, "I see myself smiling as I pass out five compliments to other people each day." Under affirmations, I wrote, "I will post blue dots and ask myself if I am doing stretch-or-shrink thinking every time I see one. I will stop exaggerating the importance of my weaknesses and quit putting myself down." Under *as if*, I wrote, "Each day I will pass out five compliments." "I will use Emotional Transfusion every day in my relations with _____." To make sure that I did this, I attached a separate page for writing down the compliments I passed out each day, recording the recipients and the reactions I received. Each day, I read over this goal sheet the first thing in the morning and again right before I went into each alpha session during the day.

Bob's Goal Sheet

Goal: I see myself as a more loving, self-confident person.

Visualization: I will picture myself smiling as I give compliments to five other people each day.

Affirmations: 1. I am loving and self-confident.
2. I am worthy of the love of other people.

Cognitive Restructuring:
1. I will use blue dots to discern when I am doing stretch-or-shrink thinking.
2. I will stop exaggerating my weaknesses and quit putting myself down.

Acting As If:
1. I will pass out five compliments to others each day.
2. I will use Emotional Transfusion each day to better my relationships with _____ .

Feedback:
   Date:
Person Complimented   *Their Reaction*

1.
2.
3.
4.
5.

   I practiced the visualizations, often choosing whom I would compliment and what I would say. Because I was staying in the house so much, this was a real challenge until I discovered I could compliment others over the phone. I could even offer compliments to business associates! Sometimes the reaction was a surprised silence on the other end of the line, but other people frequently said, "Thanks, Bob, that's good to know." And still others responded with a compliment in kind. Every time I wrote down these responses, it was like giving myself another "attaboy!" I was beginning to discover I liked feeling good about myself. These good feelings made it easier to correct my cognitive distortions about myself.

Adding New Goals

   After only a week, I had made such progress I decided to begin working on a second goal while continuing to work on the first. It's really up to you to decide when you want to start working on more than one goal, but I would suggest you allow at least a week to ten days of daily programming and acting *as if* on your first goal alone. And you may need to continue to work on it along with other goals for as long as a year. Again, it is up to you to decide when you feel you have achieved that goal and can stop working on it. Some goals can be completed in three to four months. To make goals stick, I would suggest working on them for at least thirty days.

As you begin working on many goals, you may eventually realize that all are melding into one big goal—to become the person you want to be. This is what happened to me. After beginning with my goal of becoming a happier, more confident person, I began working on a second goal of desensitizing myself to my phobia. All of a sudden I was starting to have wonderful, loving thoughts about myself and others. And for the first time in years, my daily diarrhea was gone. I became so excited at seeing results and no longer working *against* myself that I began to set goals in all areas of my life.

One day I decided to set a goal of bettering my golf game. Within a few months my handicap dropped from eighteen to nine. Next I set a goal for my career. While at alpha, I had realized that being an executive head-hunter allowed me a safe, comfortable existence, but my business was no longer growing. Furthermore, it no longer challenged me. Now I saw something that did excite me very much: if I became a public speaker, I could tell everyone how to use the unconscious to bring about all these wonderful things just as was happening for me.

But could I really become a professional speaker? I was the one whose throat closed up every time I faced a crowd. I had a hard time believing I could achieve this goal. But I broke up the acting *as if* into increments. I decided I could join Toastmasters International to learn public speaking skills and help me control my nervousness. I could join other speakers' associations. I could read and study. When I acted out these instructions, it wasn't long before I was winning blue ribbons at Toastmasters meetings. Then I began to get invitations to tell of my experiences before other groups. People actually liked to hear *me*, the man who "just couldn't face a crowd."

The Payoff in My Physical and Spiritual Goals

Next I decided to work on one of the physical fitness goals I had written down. I was thirty pounds overweight. My cholesterol and triglyceride levels were dangerously high. I was taking medication for high blood pressure. My goal was to be in excellent physical condition. I started visualizing myself as physically fit. I began jogging. I cut out foods like salt, sugar, red meat, and alcohol and found it easy to enjoy well-balanced meals. I saw myself living a life of health.

Within a few months I was able to jog fifteen miles a week. I lost twenty-four pounds. My cholesterol and triglyceride levels returned to a normal range. When I went to my doctor he told me I no longer had to take blood pressure medication. I had made big headway toward reaching my goal. I still continue to work on this one every day.

One area of goal-setting that was hard for me was the spiritual area. Now I know that I was confusing the word "spiritual" with the word "religious." I thought being spiritual meant living by a lot of religious rules and being punished for breaking them—which in itself was a misapprehension about religion. Since I already believed that I was a failure, being spiritual didn't seem like anything that would benefit me.

Nevertheless, I obediently set myself a goal of becoming more spiritual. And I found that this was one goal I didn't have to work on so hard. Whenever I went into alpha, I would feel a loving force within me, which made it possible for me to change. Gradually I began to realize that everyone else had this same universal, loving spirit. I resolved to deepen this knowledge of my spiritual self further through meditation. Eventually this goal was the one that melded all my goals into one. It made it truly possible for me to remain free of anxiety under all circumstances.

The "Impossible Goal"

Then one day my unconscious popped up with what I felt was truly an unbelievable goal. I had a burning desire to tell people all over the world—far beyond the realm of public speaking—how they could overcome the effects of anxiety and find this wonderful new way to live that I had discovered. My unconscious told me that the way to do that was to write a book. But how could I act out this goal? I was not a writer!

Even so, I wrote down my goal. I visualized myself holding a book with my name on it. I affirmed that I was going to write it. And lo and behold, at the Toastmasters meeting, I met Pauline. She was already the author of five published self-help books, and she had a deep interest in writing other books that would help people. When she heard me speak about my experience with panic, *she* asked *me* if I was interested in collaborating on a book!

I believe that my burning desire and my visualizing and affirming attracted the forces that were necessary to cause this meeting. Even when you think something seems impossible, you may be able to accomplish what you wish if your desire is strong enough.

Tips for Achieving Your Goals

Now that you know the basics for how to select and write out your goals, study these tips for how to achieve them:

1. *Be specific about how you will act out your goal.* Ask yourself how your actions will manifest what you desire. If your goal is to become more loving, write down the specifics. Will you be hugging people more often? Will you be doing things to help others, such as visiting an old folks' home or tutoring underachieving children? Will you use rational thinking when someone says things that hurt you so that you can still react with love? Write down what you will do and say.

   If your goal is to treat your children better, you might write, "I will smile at my children. I will build them up with five compliments every day. I will react with patience when they spill the milk. I will tell them I love them." The more specific you are, the easier it is to act *as if*. And the more specific your actions are, the clearer is the message to your unconscious that the new you is different from the old. Eventually it will believe that the new you is the real you and send you the feelings and thoughts that are harmonious with your actions.

2. *Share your goals only with people who will support you and encourage you to achieve them.* One raised eyebrow on the face of someone who is very important to you could throw ice water on your burning desire and reduce your self-confidence to ashes. Oddly enough, some family members are the very ones who cannot be objective about your ability to achieve a goal. Either keep your goals to yourself or share them only with those you know will believe in you.

3. *Set a time limit on achieving your goal only when you must,* such as when you are trying to lose weight. Always allow yourself enough time so that it seems believable that you can achieve it. Changing a habit like nail-biting or smoking usually takes thirty days of programming and acting out. But don't give up if it takes you longer. Be aware that your subconscious will change you if you continue to work on the goal.

   Be careful not to compare your progress to others'. To become more loving and caring may take you six months. Another person may be able to do it in three. Just look at your own successes and relish how far you've come. Pat yourself on the back for what *you* have done. Keep working on the long-term goal.

"Attaboys!" and "Oops!"

4. *Always associate good feelings with your goals.* It is going to feel wonderful when you stop craving cigarettes or start communicating with your children rather than yelling at them. As you are visualizing yourself in this new way, enjoy the thrill of success by reviewing what you have accomplished. Make your visualization as detailed as possible, including the smells, colors, and exuberant feelings. In this way, you give yourself some "attaboys!" that encourage you to keep up the good work.

5. *It's all right to make a mistake.* We've talked about this before. Recognize that when you're working to achieve a goal, it is entirely possible you will make a mistake. Don't let it worry you. And don't be discouraged by detours. Every treasure map has some misleading markings that may cause you to take wrong turns off the

main road that leads to the buried chest. But don't give up. Remember, a detour always leads back to the main road if you keep on going. Focus on the end result—the goal—and not the detours. Give yourself permission to take whatever detours you must take to get where you're going.

In the past, whenever I tried to set a goal, I always gave up the minute I got off the track. "I'm going in the wrong direction. There's no way I can get where I want to go, so I might as well stop trying," I told myself. Then one day a friend reminded me that a torpedo doesn't travel in a straight line either. It may veer off to the left, then to the right, but it always corrects itself and connects with its target. Why? Because its goal is programmed into it. We can be the same kind of goal-seeking devices if we choose to be.

6. *Keep your attention on your goals by reading them daily before going into alpha.* Carry your goal book with you at all times and refer to it often to keep you on track. Frequent reminders that you are working on goals will help you take the one step at a time that is necessary to make progress.

Checklist for Your Goal List

As you're writing down your goals, ask yourself the following questions to see whether they are truly goals or merely wishes:

1. Do I have a burning desire to accomplish this goal?
2. Is it believable?
3. If not, can I break it into monthly, weekly, daily,

or hourly increments that will make it believable?

4. Have I phrased it in a positive rather than a negative manner?
5. Can I see myself actually accomplishing this goal?
6. Can I associate strong positive feelings with the goal?
7. Can I affirm that I have reached the goal?
8. Do I care enough to act *as if* this goal has already been accomplished in my life?
9. Have I been specific in writing down how I will achieve this goal?
10. Have I made a commitment to achieve this goal?

Buried Treasure

If I were to write a modern-day fairy tale, it would go something like this: once there was a young man who had many talents but who lived far below his capabilities. It was as if a wicked witch had put a spell on him so that he had to live just the way he saw himself—and he saw himself as inferior, a failure, and a fraud. This young man wanted happiness, riches, and good feelings about himself, but the harder he tried to get them, the worse he felt.

Finally, the young man's stress became so overwhelming that he developed panic attacks. He became so miserable that it appeared that he might even lose his life. "I wish that I were able to leave the house without having a panic attack. I wish that I could feel at ease with other people and enjoy going to restaurants and plays. I wish that I could excel in my work and be a success," he often said. "But every time I try to do any of those things, I fail. If I have to live in this misery, I might as well do away with myself.''

How the poor young man wished his life would change! But nothing happened until one day he found a treasure map. This was no yellowed, hand-written paper buried in a tree stump. Instead, it was a book that told him how to set goals to make his wishes come true. When the young man perceived that this knowledge was indeed a real treasure map, he lost no time in following the directions. His search wasn't always easy. Sometimes he lost the way and had to restudy the map. But he did not give up. He had a burning desire to reach the treasure and make it his own. And one day, he did find it. He became free of his panic attacks. He found enjoyment in going wherever he wanted, whether it was far or near. And he found success in his work.

That young man was none other than myself. After I conquered my phobia through using goals, I discovered I could use the same techniques to help me in my career. At the time, I was placing mostly secretaries and bookkeepers with companies for a fee. Then I set a goal for financial success and wrote out the ways I would achieve it. When I went to alpha I became aware that if I could place mostly executives rather than secretaries, I could make much higher fees. So I acted *as if* by associating myself with a national executive search firm for a year to learn how to recruit executives. I began using visualizations and affirmations before I made my calls. I also affirmed that I was worthy of financial success and competent to do the work.

After a year, I set up my own executive search firm. Within three years my income had far surpassed what I would have believed possible. I bought a Mercedes and went off to Europe on vacation. The spell that the witch of low self-esteem had placed on me was gone.

By setting your goals, you, too, can select exactly the

treasure *you* want, whether it is riches, love, health, or freedom from anxiety. To find it, you draw and follow a road map made up of goals that tells you the way. If you are persistent, you will reach your destination. And you will enjoy your treasure the rest of your life.

In the next few chapters I will be helping you draw road maps for various specific physical, mental, and spiritual treasures that will make it possible for you to become more calm. And after that, I will tell you how goal-setting led to a new way of life for me that is far more precious than gold, silver, or jewels.

PART II

Finding Life Plus

CHAPTER 10

~~~~~~

The Physical Fitness Goal

Before I went to a psychologist, I thought my panic attacks were purely a physical problem. Something was drastically wrong with me, and I wanted medication to make me well. After I discovered that my improper reactions toward stress were causing my body to become aroused, I swung to the opposite conclusion. I decided that the only thing I needed to do was to train my unconscious to react differently toward the stressors in my life. I thought I was primarily a mind, and only incidentally did I have a body.

I was wrong. I did not *have* a body. I *was* a body as much as I was a mind. I have since discovered that the pathway to getting over anxiety has two-way traffic. When you suffer from panic disorders, you need to do cognitive restructuring. But it is also important to become physically fit.

The Anatomy of Your Mental Dysfunction

Scientists know that the gene pool of the human species has not changed in fifty thousand years. Essentially we have the same brain that our prehistoric ancestors had. Although we can think rationally with our cortex, the more primitive limbic system of the brain regulates our body temperature, rate of blood flow, and levels of adrenaline and corticosteroids—all of which come into play during a panic attack.

The limbic system, similar to the brain that completely rules the lives of animals, processes information received through the five senses. It sends some of the information about what we see, smell, hear, taste, and feel to the cortex so that we can make rational interpretations. But most of this information is sent to the hypothalamus, the part of the brain that operates like the thermostat that regulates your home furnace. When the hypothalamus receives a signal of danger from the limbic brain, it can increase your blood flow, make your salivary glands dry up, or order your stomach to empty its contents, among a host of other physical symptoms. After the limbic brain senses danger, the hypothalamus turns on a fight or flight response within one-fourth to one-half of a second.

When you see another auto almost sideswipe your fender or sense that you are losing your fiancée's affections or perceive your boss treating you unfairly, you cannot react like a caveman. You cannot obey the limbic brain's command to hit the offending driver or drag your loved one by the hair into the cave or bop your boss over the head. So your rational brain—the cortex—countermands the instructions. If you could take action, your body would pass through the alarm stage, resolve the emergency, and return to normal. But the more frequently you refuse to act, the more frantically the limbic brain signals the hypothalamus to react. You begin functioning in the chronic state of arousal known as the resistance stage. Your body systems remain tense. And if this stage goes on too long, your body reaches the exhaustion stage. The result is *psychosomatic* diseases such as migraines, colitis, ulcers, diarrhea, backaches, and anxiety attacks. The illness is real. You have real pain and an actual disease process, but the illness is *caused by your mind!*

The cortex does have some influence over the limbic system. That is why you can affect the limbic system through going into alpha and reprogramming with visualizations and affirmations. The limbic brain does not know the difference between a visualization of yourself looking calm and happy and an actual experience of happiness. It simply receives the message as reality.

When I used visualizations, I not only made headway in desensitizing myself to my fear of going outside; I also ended my colitis. I still had the same amount of stress in my life, but I fooled my limbic brain. I created *eustress* (stress disarmed by a return to a resting state) out of the situations that affected me. Gradually I began to see that *by setting goals to make physical changes as well as mental ones, I could double the rate of my progress*. My body and mind would be working together.

How the Body Affects the Brain

The reason I have a goal-setting chapter on physical fitness is not so that you can develop bulging muscles or a beautiful body. It is because when you are functioning under par physically, your body can create the same symptoms of anxiety that your mind does.

A case in point was Cindy's friend Kathy. As a travel agent, Kathy spent a good part of her working time flying around the world investigating the most famous tourist attractions. She was wined and dined by resort directors from the Côte d'Azur to Tahiti. But her job wasn't all bon voyage parties. She also had to soothe clients who became screaming ogres every time a hotel reservation was lost or an airline flight canceled.

In fact, Kathy received promotions simply because she had an excellent track record for changing roaring lions into purring kittens. Kathy had always been able to react calmly to the angriest clients. But suddenly she found herself snapping back at them. She didn't understand what was happening.

"I just can't seem to keep my cool anymore," Kathy told her boss. "By the middle of the afternoon I'm so tired my entire body is shaking. Sometimes I feel like I'm going to pass out." When Kathy tried eating candy bars for quick energy, she felt even worse. One day she answered an irate customer with the same verbal abuse he was handing her. He was an important client, and she lost him. That's when Kathy went to the doctor.

"You've got hypoglycemia—low blood sugar." he told her. "For some reason your body is producing too much insulin, the hormone that breaks down sugars and starches. Low blood sugar causes trembling, weakness, and hunger. But eating candy bars can't raise your level of blood sugar. In fact, candy is just about the worst thing you could have eaten. You need a carefully balanced diet instead."

When Kathy started paying attention to nutrition, her blood sugar level returned to normal and so did her composure at the office. Once more she had her difficult clients purring.

"It's amazing how I can stand up under pressure and be so much more tactful when my body feels okay," Kathy said. Were her temper flare-ups caused by mental anxiety or were they the result of a physical disability? Were her fears of blacking out caused by her body or her mind? Undoubtedly the stress of dealing with angry clients played its part, but so did the oversupply of insulin. She needed to learn how to use her unconscious to relax when dealing with demanding customers, but the real key to eliminating her shakiness and fussiness was eating the right foods.

What Is Physical Fitness?

Physical fitness means soundness of body and mind. I would go one step farther and say that it means being able to function at the optimal level for your age. Your goal should be to feel good, enjoy life, and be as full of energy as you can be. It means being interested in the world around you.

Most people don't know how physically fit they are because they rarely go to a doctor except when they are sick. When you set a goal for physical fitness, you need to know how you compare with the norms. So your first step should be to go to a fitness center that specializes in preventive medicine and ask to be tested for fitness. If you do not have access to such a center, then go to your family doctor. Indicate that you are interested in preventing illness, and don't accept a reply like "Well, you've got a few little minor things that won't bother you too much as long as you take these pills."

Ask your doctor to check not only your weight, pulse rate, and urine; see that you receive exhaustive blood chemistry and stress tests. When you get the results, write down the numbers or ask for a copy of the reports. Ask about any variations from the norm. If you don't understand the terms your doctor uses, insist on full explanations.

If you are having anxiety, you will probably learn some

things about your body that need changing, and you will want to set goals for relaxing, exercising, and improving your nutrition.

The Minor Illness Goal

If you have a minor illness, such as frequent headaches or nervous stomach, your first priority will be to get over it. First, be sure that your doctor has ruled out any organic reason for the illness. Then make a goal sheet like this one for tension headache:

Goal: My head feels perfectly normal.

Visualizations:
1. I picture myself with a relaxed look on my face at work and at home.
2. I visualize myself refusing requests that will cause me to overwork.
3. I see myself being able to participate in hobbies that I have avoided because I have not felt like doing them.

Affirmations:
1. My head feels perfectly normal. I can do any activity I want.
2. I am worthy of the love of others even when I refuse their requests.

Cognitive Restructuring:
1. Negative focusing: I will change my attitude of thinking I am unable to do things to an attitude of being perfectly able.
2. White-is-black thinking. I will restructure so that I stop

predicting that I will have a headache whenever I have to be with certain people.

. Fictional fantasies. I will stop thinking that something is wrong with me and therefore I am bound to have lots of headaches.

Acting As If:

. I will do deep breathing and go into alpha for relaxation several times a day.

. I will study assertiveness training so that I can refuse other people's requests in an objective manner.

How to Acquire a Burning Desire for Fitness

If you have a burning desire to get over some minor illness, by all means set your goal and work on it. Most people will find that they can stick with a goal like that because they have the motivation to work on it. But when I talk about setting a goal for overall physical fitness, their eyes glaze over, they look the other way, and mumble, "I haven't got time to exercise," or "I'm just not the type to jog," or "Carrots never did a thing for me."

This is irrational thinking. You could be under the influence of *mistaken identity*—telling yourself that because of your low self-esteem you're not worth the effort it takes to exercise. Or you could be thinking in *fictional fantasies:* "I have all these physical problems. Therefore I function below par and there's nothing I can do about it."

How do you build up the fire under your desire to exercise and eat right when it's clearly lukewarm? Consider these facts:

1. You will have fewer anxiety-producing illnesses if you achieve physical fitness.

2. You can have a new and exciting lifestyle if you are functioning at optimal levels of health. Wouldn't it be great to be able to go places and do things like those people you've always envied? You can, if you set a goal to become physically fit and then commit yourself to achieving it.

   Once you start working on your goal, you will feel so much better that you will be motivated to continue.
3. Your unconscious will make it easier to exercise and eat right if you program it with visualizations and affirmations.

How I Worked on the Physical Fitness Goal

I had a burning desire to become physically fit for two main reasons. First, I realized that my physical condition was adding to the symptoms of anxiety that I was experiencing. Second, my doctor informed me that my blood pressure and levels of cholesterol and triglycerides were dangerously high. I was well aware that my parents had both had heart attacks while in their fifties. I also knew that a lot of people were reducing the risk of heart disease through jogging and other kinds of aerobic conditioning. The more I thought about that, the more I wanted to do it.

I quickly realized, however, that I needed to do some cognitive restructuring. Every time I thought about jogging, my unconscious told me, "You can't do that." So I went into alpha and asked myself why I thought I couldn't do it. Because of my foot. When I was a child the doctors had told my mother I wouldn't be able to participate in sports. My unconscious took all that in and all my life I incorporated their opinions into my fictional fantasies. "You can't jog. That's just the way you are."

So before writing anything down on my goal sheet, I thought about the fact that I could dance and enjoy it. I could play golf and have a wonderful time. There really was no reason at all why I couldn't jog if I wanted to! I didn't have to be a perfectionist and jog a twenty-six-mile marathon. I could jog to the level of my abilities.

Here's what I put on my goal sheet:

Goal: I am able to jog fifteen miles a week.

Visualizations:
1. I picture myself jogging and enjoying it.
2. I see myself breathing easily as I jog through beautiful parts of town.

Affirmations:
1. I enjoy being able to jog.
2. I feel perfectly comfortable while jogging.
3. Jogging is making my heart strong.
4. Jogging is lowering my blood pressure and reducing my levels of cholesterol and triglycerides.

Cognitive Restructuring:
1. Perfectionism: It's okay to risk a new activity, and if I don't do it right at first, that's okay, too.
2. Fictional fantasies: I will change my attitude from thinking I can't jog because "that's just the way I am" to "Of course I can jog."
3. Mistaken identity: Despite any past mistakes or failures, I believe that I am worth saving from a heart attack. I am worth the effort it takes to learn to jog.

Acting As If:
1. I will take a stress test.
2. I will read books on jogging that tell me how to start slowly and gradually increase my endurance.

3. I will follow the charts that show me how far to walk or jog each week.
4. I will record how far I have gone each day.

I have to admit that the first few weeks of walking and jogging were challenging. I couldn't even jog a whole block without gasping for breath. But I kept on visualizing and affirming. I kept on telling myself I was worth the effort. I recorded each week's progress on my goal sheet. Finally, I jogged two whole miles without any walking, and I basked in a heady feeling of accomplishment all day.

After three months of gradually increasing the distance I went, I could jog three miles. I was so excited about my progress that I decided I would like to participate in the ten-kilometer Azalea Run in Dallas. I had never jogged ten kilometers, but I worked through my perfectionist thinking and told myself it was all right if I didn't make it to the finish line. I knew that I would enjoy the springtime scenery, if nothing else.

On the morning of the run, I felt a surge of excitement as I lined up with about three thousand others at the starting point. Then as we jogged out along the Turtle Creek parkways with their gorgeous azalea gardens, my feet just seemed to take over. I don't know whether it was the result of being with the crowd or the high I got from the beautiful flowering shrubs, but I jogged the whole way. I even forged up the steep hill at the very end, and it looked as if it went straight up! I felt wonderful! Now I make it a point to participate in every run I can find.

Incidentally, I received positive feedback from the Azalea Run by mentioning it in a motivational speech I gave before a group of young singles a week later. I told them I had thought I would never be able to jog because of my disability. But then I held up my Azalea Run T-shirt as proof that I had jogged ten kilometers, and the audience cheered and clapped. What a lot of positive strokes that gave me! I felt eager to work on more physical fitness goals.

The Giant Eraser

Think of physical fitness as a giant eraser that can relieve you of tension and stress. It can wipe clean a long list of physical problems you collect from living a sedentary life. A brisk thirty-minute walk after a hard day at work produces more relaxation than a half hour with a cocktail at a bar. The runner's high you get from jogging three miles makes it easy not to answer Mr. Negative. You can improve your digestive system, sleep more easily, concentrate better on your work, and diminish back pain and depression if you aim for a goal of overall physical fitness. As you trim your body, you enhance your self-esteem, too. What more could you ask? Go for it!

Major corporations are now investing millions of dollars to provide fitness equipment for their employees. They recognize that fit workers miss fewer days of work, produce more, and get along better with each other. Exxon, PepsiCo, Johnson & Johnson, Xerox, and Electronic Data Systems are only a few of the enlightened corporations that recognize that their employees are bodies as much as minds.

My friend Marilyn, the only female attorney in a prestigious law firm, discovered how important fitness was. To hold her position, Marilyn felt pressured to accomplish more than all the young male lawyers. She pushed herself so hard that she began to have terrible headaches. When her work started to suffer because of them, she went to the doctor. He discovered that she was grinding her teeth while she slept. Bruxism, as this problem is called, is caused by nervous tension.

Marilyn asked me to teach her how to relax, so I taught her the Five Basic Principles. At the same time, she started taking long walks every evening and eating three good meals every day. Within a few weeks, her headaches were gone.

Relaxation, exercise, and nutrition erased Marilyn's physical and emotional problems. They can do the same for you.

The Relaxation Goal

We've already talked a lot about how to go into alpha and relax. If you haven't already been doing this, set a goal of learning to become more relaxed. Here is a sample goal sheet:

Goal: I feel perfectly relaxed at all times.

Visualizations:
1. I picture myself performing at work in a perfectly calm manner with a smile on my face.
2. I see myself being perfectly calm in my relationships with my friends and family.
3. I will use Emotional Transfusion to overcome feelings of nervousness when I _____ .

Affirmations:
1. My heartbeat is steady, and my breathing is slow and deep.
2. I feel completely relaxed at all times.

Cognitive Restructuring:
1. Fictional fantasies: I will change my belief that I am a nervous person and there's nothing I can do about it to one that I can be calm and relaxed.

2. Mistaken identity: I am a person who deserves to take the time to make myself feel relaxed.

Acting As If:
1. I will use the Blue Dot Technique to discern when I am feeling tense.
2. I will go into alpha six times a day and rest for five minutes before trying to program myself.
3. I will do deep breathing whenever I feel myself becoming anxious.
4. I will reserve at least one afternoon a week for developing a hobby I enjoy.
5. I will go to bed on time so that I allow myself an adequate number of hours to sleep.

Tips for Working on Your Relaxation Goal

• When you are doing your cognitive restructuring, be aware that when you are depressed about a terrible loss, such as a job, you may be telling yourself some pretty bad things about yourself. You may try to blot out your grief by sleeping away all of your spare time or hitting the bottle or running around twenty-four hours a day in senseless activities. Realize that what you really seek is the self-esteem that you have lost. Work on mistaken identity and give yourself permission to seek good things for yourself. Sleeping too much, drinking, or exhausting yourself will only harm your body and increase your feelings of anxiety.

The solution may be to erase the fictional fantasy thinking that "The only way I can stand this pain is to escape it with sleep, alcohol, or activity" and replace it with the rational thought, "Yes, I have suffered a lot of pain, but so have a lot of other people. They got over it and so will I. I am still a person of self-worth. I deserve to have a healthy body."

- Don't try to relax by oversleeping, either. Doctors now believe that most people require no more than seven to eight hours of sleep each night. If you take long naps the next day in addition to lying in bed eight hours, you may end up feeling *less* relaxed. Why? Your body requires exercise as well as rest to function as it was created. Even the small amounts of exercise you get by simply standing or moving around are better than staying in bed. A person who has been inactive for three days has lost 5 percent of his strength, and only exercise and activity can undo the damage, say exercise specialists.

Exercise: What Kind?

Any regular exercise routine is good for you, but it makes especially good sense for anxious people to aim for aerobic conditioning. The articulated goal for aerobic exercise is to raise the level of the heart rate for sustained periods of time so as to strengthen the heart and vascular system and prevent coronary heart disease. But aerobic conditioning has a double payoff for the anxious. You not only strengthen your heart, but you also enable your body to use oxygen more efficiently. Deep breathing helps maintain a correct pH balance. (See Chapter 5.)

If you decide to do some aerobic conditioning, you will not be alone. Sweat suits are now a fashion item. Jogging shoes are a status symbol. Doctors are cautiously crediting renewed interest in strenuous exercise as one of the reasons why the death rate from heart disease is going down.

Jogging isn't the only way to exercise aerobically. I know

a schoolteacher who uses her class break to pedal a stationary bicycle in the teachers' lounge for twenty minutes every day. I have friends who join bicycle clubs and take hundred-mile fun caravans over the weekends. The YMCAs have swim groups and aerobic dancing classes. Just plain walking is one of the very best ways to exercise.

Most authorities believe that you should increase your heart rate through performing some kind of aerobic exercise at the proper intensity for your age and physical condition for at least twenty minutes three to four times a week. Be sure to take a stress test to learn whether it is safe for you to do aerobic exercises before you begin.

Don't forget, however, that strength and flexibility are other important aspects of being fit. In 1984, the President's Council on Physical Fitness and the National Fitness Foundation sponsored nationwide tests to see how fit American adults were. Many proficient joggers who took the tests received only silver medals for overall fitness. Although they qualified for the gold medal in the step-up test that measured heart and pulse rate under strenuous exercise, they did not qualify in push-ups, arm hangs, and curl-ups. They had neglected to exercise for strength and flexibility.

So, in addition to working on aerobic conditioning, do some regular loosening-up exercises every day. Punctuate long, easy stretches with deep, easy breathing. If you don't feel motivated to do them on your own, join a spa or attend one of the many exercise classes that are available in most communities.

Sample Goal Sheet for Exercising

Goal: I see myself becoming physically fit through exercise.

Visualizations:

1. I picture myself jogging (or swimming, jumping rope, or some other activity) and enjoying it.
2. I see myself doing flexibility exercises with pleasure.
3. I picture my heart beating perfectly normally. I see my arteries looking like transparent pipes completely free of atherosclerotic plaque, so that the blood flows freely through them into and out of my heart.
4. I see my face glowing with health.

Affirmations:

1. I enjoy doing my exercises every morning.
2. My heart is becoming healthier. My ability to breathe deeply is increasing.

Cognitive Restructuring:

1. Refusing the positives: I will stop telling myself that exercise, which will help me overcome anxiety, is boring or dangerous for me. I will go for the good things available to me.
2. Fictional fantasies: I will stop telling myself that I am "just lazy" and therefore unable to jog.
3. Mistaken identity: I will stop thinking I am unworthy of taking the time required to exercise.

Acting As If:

1. I will read books that inform me of the kinds of exercise that will be best for me.
2. I will set up an exercise schedule for every day and keep a log of my progress.

Another Reason for Physical Fitness

Like little acorns, the minor ailments that go along with anxiety can turn into something mighty if you continue to let them grow. My friend Tom, whom you met in Chapter 9, refused to work on physical fitness and better family relationships; he said he was too old to change. He rationalized by saying, "That's just the way life is." Eventually a bleeding ulcer got his attention. Tom then set a goal of learning to relax and achieve fitness. But his body had already paid the toll.

If you do not break the cycle of anxiety, bracing, a sedentary lifestyle, and poor eating habits, your high blood pressure can grow into a stroke or a heart attack. Your smoking can lead to cancer. And your nervous stomach can turn into an ulcer. Uproot those little seedlings before they send down huge taproots. Set your goal to become physically fit, and then use my Five Basic Principles to make it easy to relax and exercise.

CHAPTER 11

∿∿

Physical Goals: How to Eat Right and Control Your Weight

I couldn't resist commenting on the breakfast one of my fellow Toastmasters ordered at a meeting one morning. A fried egg and bacon swimming in grease, four pieces of toasted white bread with jelly, and a generous portion of hash brown potatoes, it was the typical American breakfast—fattening and low in nutritional value.

"Beth, I've just got to say this to you," I began. "Do you really know what you're putting into your body with that breakfast?" I knew that Beth had received an important promotion at the bank the past year. She complained that her desk job gave her no time for exercise and that she was feeling fatigued and on edge. She was also putting on weight. But she only laughed at what I said.

"I know it isn't the best for me, Bob," she said. "But don't worry. I usually eat breakfast at the company cafeteria, and then I just order two biscuits and gravy." Inwardly I groaned. The amount she regularly ate was less, but the number of calories packed into those smaller portions was still far too high for someone trying to lose weight. And for someone who was fatigued and on edge, the nutritional value (empty-calorie white flour and animal fat) was poor.

If you are overweight, I urge you to set a goal of losing the number of pounds that will put you back within the normal range for your age, height, and bone structure. Being trim will do more than make you more physically fit. You will look better and feel so good about yourself that it will be easier to avoid the distorted thinking that compounds stress.

You may be thinking: easier said than done. Almost everyone wants to shed a few pounds. Every bookstore you see is loaded with diet books. Hardly a women's magazine is published that doesn't contain at least one article on how to lose weight. Yet, wherever you go, people are complaining about their oversized hips, bulging stomachs, and fleshy arms.

The problem is that most people just don't know how to shed pounds. They know a lot about fad diets and misinformation, but they don't know how they can use my Five Basic Principles and the three keys to weight control.

Test Your Weight-Control IQ

Do you have some misconceptions about the best way to lose weight? Test your knowledge by answering the following questions true or false.

1. A calorie is a measure of quantity of fat.
   False. A calorie is a heat unit—the amount of heat required to raise the temperature of one kilogram of

water from zero degrees Centigrade to one degree. The term "calorie" is used to measure the amount of fuel within a quantity of food which can be burned in the body's metabolic system to produce energy. If the food you eat contains too many calories and your body does not burn them all, then the surplus is stored as fat.

2. You will lose weight and be healthy if you count the caloric content of the food you eat and limit the total to 1200 a day.

   False. The quality of the calories is just as important as the quantity. You can lose weight on a 1200-calorie diet, but you will not be healthy if the 1200 calories come from two chocolate sundaes with whipped cream. For good health, your body needs protein, fiber, minerals, and vitamins, which you would not get from two sundaes.

3. A baked potato contains more calories than ice cream.

   False. A dish of ice cream contains 269 while a baked potato contains only 100. The potato also provides minerals and dietary fiber. Potatoes and other starchy foods such as cereals have a bad reputation. But it is the additions put on these foods—calorie-heavy butter and sour cream on potatoes, or cream and sugar on cereal—that do the damage.

4. Skipping breakfast is a good way to lose weight.

   False. When you skip breakfast, your body lacks the fuel it needs for your morning routines. Without breakfast, you are likely to sag at midmorning. Then you will drink coffee to feel better. But the caffeine in the coffee also causes insomnia, restlessness, heart palpitations, and tremors that complicate the lives of anxious people.

5. If you weigh two hundred pounds and walk one hour at

the rate of four and a half miles per hour, you burn up 540 calories.

True. And if you weigh two hundred pounds and run at the rate of five and a half miles per hour, you will burn up an astounding 876 calories. Slow swimming (twenty yards per minute) burns up 392 and moderate tennis 565.

6. You must burn 3500 calories to lose one pound of fat.

True. Although that sounds like a lot of calories, you don't have to burn them all up at one time. If you weigh two hundred pounds and you walk briskly for only half an hour a day, you will have burned up a pound of fat within two weeks. (One pound of fat will be gone regardless of how much you eat, but if you also take in more calories then you need, you will be adding pounds at the same time. If you are on this kind of seesaw, you may never notice the pound you lost.)

7. When you are working on a weight loss plan, it is a good idea to weigh yourself every day.

True. By all means chart your weight and see yourself losing pounds. Your success will encourage you to continue. But don't be discouraged if you fail to lose anything on some days. It is normal for your weight to fluctuate, and it is also normal to stay on a plateau at times. If you don't see progress weighing yourself every day, or if you sense yourself getting anxious about it, try stepping on the scales only once a week. Then results will be more evident.

8. Regularly reminding yourself not to eat fattening foods is a good idea.

False. Reminding your unconscious with a negative statement like "I am not going to eat cake and cookies any more" is a good way to psych your boss into tempting you to eat them. Instead, affirm "I enjoy fresh fruit and vegetables more than cake and cookies."

9. Rewarding yourself each time you lose a set amount of weight will help you lose more weight.

True. Remember operant conditioning? You can increase your willingness to stay on a weight reduction plan if you treat yourself to a reward each time you achieve a minor weight loss goal. Go to a movie, buy yourself a good book, or enjoy an afternoon of golf. But don't buy yourself a sundae and erase the benefit of a good half hour of walking.

Three Keys to Weighing What You Want

If you answered all these questions correctly, congratulations! You are probably slender, pleasantly proportioned, and not too concerned about weight loss. If you didn't, you are like most Americans. You flounder between ignorance and myth. You may pin your hopes on eating nothing but grapefruit or consuming everything you want. Or like many people, the famous and the unknown, you may put yourself on the freeway to bizarre behavior and nervous tension by combining too many diet pills with fasting routines.

Successful weight control means first losing the pounds you need to lose and second, *keeping them off for the rest of your life*. The three keys I have discovered for doing this are to count calories, eat right, and exercise enough.

The First Key—Counting Calories

After I had desensitized myself to the point of enjoying being with other people again, I decided I wanted to lose my paunch and look good. My doctor's report gave me further motivation. I weighed in at 176 rather than the 149 that was normal for my height, so I knew that I needed to consume fewer calories. I never had really counted the number of calories in my daily meals, but I am sure that I went well over 3500. I was taking in far more than I needed for my sedentary lifestyle. I probably ate at least a thousand calories worth of ice cream every evening. Yet the books I bought on weight loss said that the total number of calories allowed on a crash diet was only 1200 per day (if that)!

I set my goal at a more sensible 1500, a level that would enable me to lose weight at a slower rate but one that did not seem so drastic to me. And because I had to follow a special diet that was low in animal fat, sugar, and salt to reduce my cholesterol and triglyceride levels, I paid special attention to the nutritional content of the foods I planned to eat.

After studying my books, I came up with a food regimen that seemed right for me. I refused to call it a diet at all. Instead, I referred to it as my Sensible Eating Plan. Here is a typical menu for one day:

My Sensible Eating Plan

	Calories
For breakfast:	
One banana blended in a food processor with two tablespoons of protein supplement and one cup of orange juice	280
Two shredded wheat biscuits with .5 percent low-fat milk	340
For lunch:	
1 8-ounce carton of yogurt	225
or tuna salad sandwich, whole wheat bread	350
or 1 serving tuna salad	254
For supper:	
brown rice and lentils, 2 to 3 cups	300 to 400

or 4 to 6 ounces of skinless chicken breast	125
or 4 to 6 ounces of broiled fish	125
two servings of broccoli, squash, carrots, or turnips	80
one apple or other fresh fruit	100

By following this basic menu, I had room to add a few snacks—vegetables, a glass of low-fat milk before bed, or fruit. Or I could add a slice or two of bread to fill in at a meal. My Sensible Eating Plan incorporated two of the three keys I needed to lose weight and keep it off—counting calories and watching nutrition.

The Second Key—Nutrition

We Americans are notorious for our fast-food, high-salt, empty-calorie eating. We don't want to worry about something called nutritional balance. It might not taste good! That's what we think because we don't know how delicious nutritious meals can be. We don't know what nutrition is, and many doctors don't either because medical schools offer few if any nutrition courses.

To figure out what your Nutrition IQ is, take this quiz:

1. A normal diet should include all the nutrients available for the body to function at the highest level. How many kinds of nutrients are there—three, five, or eight?

    Answer: Five—proteins, carbohydrates, fats, vitamins, and minerals.

2. To get the amount of protein you need, eat lots of meat. True or false?

    Answer: False. Large quantities of red meat may provide more protein than is needed, leaving the body unable to utilize all of it. If you depend largely on animal food for your protein needs, you take in too much saturated fat, which increases your cholesterol level and makes you subject to stroke and coronary heart disease.

3. Most nutritionists now recommend a diet that is (a) high in protein and low in complex carbohydrates: (b) low in protein and high in complex carbohydrates.

Answer: (b) You should eat about 60 percent carbohydrates (of which only 10 percent should originate from refined sugars), 10 to 12 percent protein, and 28 to 30 percent fat.

4. The United States Department of Agriculture's Daily Food Plan includes four food groups of which you should eat two to four servings each day. These food groups are milk, meat, vegetables and fruits, and _____ .

Answer: bread and cereal. These are high-energy carbohydrates and a better choice than refined sugar, which can increase your physical symptoms of anxiety.

5. All sugars are bad for you. True or false?

Answer: False. Concentrated sugars, such as table sugar, brown sugar, and powdered sugar, can make some people hyperactive and cause a vitamin B-12 deficiency and a decrease in important minerals. These sugars are found in processed foods, candies, and sweetened breakfast cereals. The natural sugars found in fruits, berries, dairy products, grains, vegetables, and other unprocessed foods provide energy, and these foods also contain the proteins, vitamins, minerals, and fiber that your body requires.

6. How much sugar do Americans get each year in eating processed foods such as canned foods, soft drinks, and

prepared mixes—forty pounds, seventy pounds, or ninety pounds?

Answer: seventy pounds per person per year.

7. Which of the following foods has the most sugar: a one-ounce square of fudge, a slice of apple pie, or a twelve-ounce cola drink?

Answer: The twelve-ounce cola drink, which contains seven to nine teaspoons of sugar. (The fudge contains four and a half teaspoons and the pie, seven teaspoons.)

8. Processed food provides about 75 percent of the average American's salt consumption. Which has the most salt—8.5 ounces of Heinz Beef Stew, Campbell's Cream of Celery Soup, or Kentucky Fried Chicken three-piece dinner?

Answer: Kentucky Fried Chicken, which in 1984 had 2285 mg. Heinz Beef Stew had 1272. Campbell's Cream of Celery had 930.

9. Caffeine is a good source of quick energy. True or false?

Answer: False. Although caffeine may make you more alert for a few minutes, it produces a letdown effect afterward. To avoid that, most people drink another cup of coffee. Too much caffeine leads to restlessness, overactivity, nervousness, insomnia, and excessive urination.

10. Caffeine is found only in coffee and tea. True or false.

Answer: False. Caffeine is also found in chocolate and some soft drinks.

If you didn't know the answers to these questions, you are likely eating some foods that contribute to your physical problems and your anxiety attacks. You really can't be at your optimal level of health without knowing more about nutrition.

How I Worked on the Nutrition Goal

I used to eat like most Americans: too much meat, sugar, salt, and caffeine. My favorite food was steak or good old salty hamburgers and french fries with rich ice cream for dessert. Vegetables? They were something Mother told me I should eat, but I rarely did.

When Cindy and I started studying nutrition books, we found that our impressions of a good diet were all baloney! We discovered we must eat *all five* of the major nutrients to build and repair tissues that wear out as the result of living and to provide energy. If we slight any one of the five classes, we may have physical problems, including being overweight and feeling tired.

It didn't take us long to discover that we were eating too much red meat, french fries, butter, white bread, and sweets and that we were neglecting whole grains, fruits, and vegetables. We had a long discussion about which foods we would be willing to give up. Then we decided to eat a lot more of the foods we needed. We discovered that by eating brown rice and lentils, for instance, we could get a lot of the protein we needed without eating cholesterol-high red meats.

I have to laugh now when I remember our approach to eating more vegetables. We started opening cans! When we studied the nutrition books some more, we found out that most vegetables have the highest nutritional value when they are fresh and raw. If you must cook them, you should do so in the shortest possible time and use the least amount of water so that all the vitamins and minerals won't be leached out of them. Canned vegetables are cooked at very high heat with plenty of salt, so their nutritional value is questionable.

We learned to steam vegetables or zap them into the microwave, which cooks them very quickly with little or no water. By experimenting with spices and lemon flavorings, we created delicious, wholesome, filling meals without white bread, gravies, sauces, and red meats—and without too many calories, too.

Eventually I gave up alcoholic drinks because they were full of useless and unnecessary calories and coffee because of its anxiety-producing drawbacks. The fact that I felt very tired for a few days after I stopped drinking coffee made me realize that my body had become addicted to it. But within a few days I felt better than ever. Next I cut back my refined sugar intake to practically nothing. Finally I reduced the amount of sodium in my diet.

Lately I have been experimenting with vegetarianism. Cindy bought a cookbook that explains how to make all kinds of delicious balanced meals using vegetables. We've introduced ourselves to alternative high-protein sources like tofu. We have discovered we love vegetables! And we feel great!

I am not a fanatic about being a vegetarian. I still think it's fun to go out and to eat barbeque with my friends once in a while. I am just trying to eat in such a way that I will reach my optimal level of health.

The payoff came in being able to give up my high blood pressure medication and in feeling calmer, happier, and more full of zest for life. The benefits are well worth doing without steak, alcohol, and coffee.

Your Nutrition Goal

Here is a sample goal sheet for someone who wants to start working on nutritional improvement. As you learn more about nutrition, you may want to set goals for giving up certain foods that you have determined are bad for you.

Goal: I will eat only the foods that provide the best nutrition for me.

Visualizations:
1. I see myself eating with gusto foods that I previously did not like.
2. I picture myself feeling more healthy and relaxed because I am eating correctly.

Affirmations:
1. I enjoy feeling good because I am eating balanced meals.
2. I enjoy eating _____ and _____ .

Cognitive Restructing:
1. White-is-black thinking: I will stop predicting that I will never learn to like my new way of eating.
2. "Should" and "ought" legalisms: I will recognize that I don't like certain vegetables because I am still responding as I did when I was a child. I am an adult now and can make my own decisions about what is good for me.
3. Mistaken identity: Regardless of what I have done in the past, I will realize I am worth going to a lot of trouble to learn about good nutrition and to practice it.

Acting As If:
1. I will buy a good book on nutrition and study it diligently.

2. I will plan my menus one week at a time so that I will always eat nutritiously.
3. I will begin to cut out the foods that are bad for me.

The Third Key—Exercise

Once I had mastered the first two keys—counting calories and eating nutritiously—I made a startling discovery. If you use only these two keys, your body adjusts to a lower-calorie diet and begins storing fat again! At last I understood why most people can diet successfully but fail miserably in their attempt to maintain the right weight. But there is something they can do. A regular exercise routine will prevent the body from storing fat on the lower-calorie diet.

Because I had already begun jogging, I didn't need to set up an exercise plan. But now I knew I would probably have to keep on jogging all my life. Could I really keep on using all three of these keys?

With the help of my faithful unconscious I could. Each day I went into alpha several times and visualized and affirmed myself eating right, exercising—and *enjoying it.* I programmed myself to look on my new lifestyle as an adventure. And I promised myself rewards. One of my most potent visualizations was to see myself looking wonderful in the new suit I'd seen at my favorite store. I was going to reward myself with it the minute the scales hit 149 pounds.

Like most dieters, I had days when I lost weight and other days when I didn't. But by checking my daily records, I could see that the general direction was down, not up. Within six months I lost twenty-seven pounds, purchased my new suit, and found myself receiving compliments on my improved appearance. I knew that I had accomplished a goal that most people believe is practically impossible. My self-image improved so much as a result that I could really enjoy the compliments.

At the time I am writing this book, I have maintained my weight at 149 pounds for two years. I still follow a Sensible Eating Plan and continue to study nutrition. I no longer miss my old eating habits.

Goal Sheet for Losing Weight

Goal: I will weigh the number of pounds that are normal for my height and age.

Visualizations:
1. I picture myself dressed in a swimsuit looking great at the pool.
2. I picture myself looking trim and sharp while enjoying myself at a party.
3. When mind pictures of foods that tempt me come into my consciousness, I draw a big red X over them.
4. I see my spouse (or any other special person) looking at me with pride and complimenting my appearance.

Affirmations:
1. I am getting slimmer and slimmer every day.
2. I am worthy of the effort it takes to exercise and eat sensibly.
3. I enjoy eating sensibly to make myself healthy.
4. I like the foods on my Sensible Eating Plan.

Cognitive Restructuring:
1. Perfectionism: It is all right if I slip and eat something I shouldn't. I can still go on to achieve my goal.
2. Rejectionitis: I will stop trying to make up for the loss of something by eating. I will replace the thought ''I

am going to eat this cake so I won't feel so miserable'' with ''I really miss _____ , but eating won't bring him/her/it back. I'll get over this loss. Meanwhile I choose to take good care of myself.''

3. Negative focus: I will stop telling myself that my appearance is all bad because I am overweight. I will dress attractively and focus on my good features.
4. White-is-black phenomenon: I will stop predicting that I can't lose weight.

Acting As If:

1. I will study some good books on nutrition.
2. I will consult calorie charts and plan meals that total no more than 1500 calories a day.
3. Whenever I refuse something fattening, I will write down what I have done and then reward myself.
4. I will accept the compliments that people give me for losing weight or looking good.
5. I will keep a daily chart of my progress, recording my weight gain or loss.
6. I will keep a chart of my progress in exercising.

What to Say to the Snake

I don't want you to think that I am such a superhuman that I never have temptations to eat all those steaks, french fries, and ice cream on which I have drawn big red X's in my visualizations. Sometimes I give in to the snake— usually when I am eating with friends. When this happens, I just accept the slip as a human frailty. The next morning I check myself on the scales. If I have gained, I compensate for the goodies by extra jogging. I believe it is healthier to give in now and then than to feel that I am the only person in the world who can't eat steak—and then gorge on it when my sense of deprivation goes out of control.

When tennis champ Martina Navratilova suffered a disastrous illness, she retained the celebrated nutritionist Dr. Robert Haas to help her rebuild her strength. Haas created what he called a peak performance diet, which was low in animal fats. After she defeated Chris Evert Lloyd in the Daihatsu Challenge Cup finals in Brighton, England, Haas surprised Martina with her favorite dinner—Peking duck with all the trimmings. Although this special dish had a very high fat content, Haas told Martina that an occasional cheat was nothing to worry about.

Even so, be careful about rationalizations. Right after I started on my plan, Cindy and I discovered yogurt-covered peanuts. They were delicious! The snake told us they had to be good for us. Didn't they contain yogurt, one of the most sensible and nutritionally sound foods ever created? But we soon realized that we were consuming sacks of these treats each week. Finally, we admitted to ourselves that this "sensible" food was loaded with sugar. The snake had won out and we hadn't even realized it. We had to go to alpha and place a big red X on yogurt-covered peanuts before we started losing weight again.

Eating to Compensate for Stress

When you're under more stress than usual, the temptation to eat the wrong foods is almost overpowering, as my friend Gary found out. After the airline for which he flew went broke, Gary lost his job. Unhappy that he could not find another position as a pilot, Gary made the best of his situation by buying a retail store. But the shop didn't produce the plush salary with fringe benefits to which he was accustomed. He was having to work night and day just to stay in business. Instead of eating three balanced meals each day, Gary snacked or sent out for pizza. Before he knew it he was fifty pounds overweight. He couldn't sleep at night. His heart frequently raced, and he was so nervous that he felt as if he were going to blow up.

"It just seems like everything is going wrong," he complained. Then he started using my Five Basic Principles. He learned to go into alpha and relax so that he reduced the panicky symptoms he was experiencing. He looked at himself, sought some cognitive awareness, and realized that he was suffering from rejectionitis and fictional fantasies. He was seeing the failure of the airline as a personal rejection and telling himself, "I can no longer work as a pilot, therefore my life is a mess and I might as well give up and look for satisfactions in food and alcohol." And he was predicting that his life would never be any better.

He saw that the more pounds he gained, the worse he felt about himself, and the more stress he added to his rain barrel. Gary did some cognitive restructuring by reminding himself that the airline's failure had nothing to do with his self-worth. He still deserved to take better care of himself and enjoy life in his new career. He began to affirm that he liked his new way of life. He set up a Sensible Eating Plan, began to exercise, and continued to go into alpha to relax. Gradually his weight came down, and his sleeplessness went away. As his appearance improved, he felt better about himself and found fulfillment in his new career.

Although I don't feel anxiety or depression nearly so much as I used to before I knew how to relax, I occasionally do succumb to the temptation to eat away a case of the blues. But now I buy myself frozen yogurt with banana chips instead of a chocolate sundae. The frozen yogurt has about one-third fewer calories than the 22 percent butterfat ice cream I used to eat. And the banana chips are more nutritious than the chocolate syrup.

If you're feeling low enough to go off your Sensible Eating Plan more than once or twice a week, however, you probably have some other problems in your life which you need to confront. It is not normal to feel depressed so frequently. With professional help you can work through your depression and then it will be easier to stick to a Sensible Eating Plan.

Eating Right in Public

Shortly after I put myself on my Sensible Eating Plan, I had to make a speech at a dinner meeting of a large association. Sitting at the head table, I was horrified when the waiter brought me a plate that had everything on it I shouldn't eat: prime rib, a baked potato already drenched in butter, and a salad with a heavy dressing. The program chairman who had invited me to speak sat next to me. He was almost ecstatic about the menu.

"You can't say we're not treating you first class, Bob," he said, as he dug into his juicy red meat. I didn't know how not to eat it without hurting his feelings. I swallowed a few bites of potato. Then I cut the meat up into small pieces, ate one, and pushed the rest under the potato skin. Then I mentally patted myself on the back for not eating the whole thing.

Actually, I had accomplished something next to a miracle. In the past I would have eaten every bite rather than admit I was dieting. What would people think?

Now I've learned to speak up when I am served fattening, nutritionally inadequate food. Recently when I was the speaker for a breakfast meeting, the waiter brought me the breakfast he was serving to everyone—a big serving of scrambled eggs, three greasy pieces of bacon, and a sweet roll. This time I simply sent the plate back and asked the waiter to bring me two pieces of whole wheat toast. No one said a word about my strange behavior.

Start Today

If you want to lose weight, feel better about yourself, and reduce your anxiety, don't procrastinate. Commit yourself to losing weight and write out your goal sheet. As one friend whom I helped shed pounds told me, sleeping on it burns up only 10 calories; cooling your heels just 15; and grasping at straws a mere 30. But laying the facts on the table burns up 75 and running away with the notion 100. By the time you climb the ladder of success, you will have burned enough calories to rid yourself of all the pounds you never wanted.

There are no shortcuts to successful weight loss and weight maintenance. But going on a Sensible Eating Plan and exercising is a small price to pay. By using my Five Basic Principles, you can make your new healthier lifestyle seem natural in a short period of time. You will look and feel great.

CHAPTER 12

~~~~~~

Physical Goals: Reducing Anxiety When You Have Serious Illness

A friend of my father, Eliot, seemed to be the picture of health. At sixty-one, he went to the doctor for a routine checkup and was told he had the physiological system of a forty-year-old. His pulse rate, blood pressure, and blood chemistry were all excellent. Eliot took vitamins and followed a sound diet. He lived an active life that should have kept him fit.

At sixty-two, he went to the doctor for a physical and was told he had a cancerous tumor in his colon. The surgeon removed it, assuring him that he had cut away every bit of the malignant tissue. To make doubly sure that the cancer would not spread, the surgeon advised Eliot to take a series of radiation treatments.

Eliot called me from the hospital, his voice full of worry.

"Didn't you say the surgeon told you that he got all the tumor?" I asked.

"Yes," Eliot said. "But I've never been sick a day in my life. I'm scared."

"I understand why you're scared," I said, "but worrying is the worst thing you can do. You see, when you give in to anxiety, you make any illness worse. If you can relax instead, your body's natural healing powers will take over."

"How can I relax?" Eliot protested. "I could die from that one little tumor." Eliot had always been a worrier, a real white-is-black thinker. No matter what the situation was, he always predicted the worst. We talked for a long time, but I had the feeling that Eliot hadn't heard what I was saying.

Two weeks later I received the message that Eliot was dead, not from cancer, but from his heart. His fear had been so overpowering that he had developed an arrhythmia. His heart just stopped beating.

"His anxiety is what killed him," the doctor told his wife. "Eliot simply worried himself to death."

What a waste of a man who had been like a second father to me! Despite his worrying, Eliot was a kind person and I really loved him. Poor Eliot had done negative focusing on an ailment that really was rather inconsequential after his surgery. I suspect he pictured his fear of dying so vividly that his unconscious began to carry out what it saw as an order. Eliot lost many years of life that could have been productive and enjoyable because he wouldn't stop worrying.

If you have a life-threatening disease, you may feel you have every right to be anxious. A diagnosis of cancer, heart attack, ulcer, or diabetes strikes fear into the heart of everyone. You may even realize that anxiety will make your situation worse yet feel as helpless as my friend Eliot to do anything about it.

You can, of course, get professional help for your fear.

Just talking out your anxiety with an accepting person sometimes helps you to release it. Another avenue of action is to set a goal for better health and use my Five Basic Principles. You can program your mind to let your body's natural ability to heal take over.

The Physical Connection between Stress and Disease

Current medical thinking suggests that all people have cancerous cells in their bodies from time to time which are destroyed by the immune system. But as you learned in Chapter 10, in times of great anxiety, the limbic system activates the hypothalamus, the body thermostat. When the hypothalamus calls for a fight or flight response, it also shuts down the immune system. Then cancer cells can multiply.

Doctors have strong evidence that a suppressed immune system allows cancer cells to grow. In one famous case, surgeons transplanted a kidney which they thought was perfectly healthy. As is usual in transplant surgery, the patient received immunosuppressive drugs to prevent rejection of the kidney. But within a few days, this patient had a tumorous growth in his chest. When the surgeons did exploratory surgery, they found his new kidney swollen and full of malignant cells. Cancer had already spread from the kidney to the lungs. Immediately they stopped the immunosuppressive medication, and within only a few days all the cancer disappeared! Their only explanation was that the kidney had had a few undetected cancer cells before it was transplanted. When the immune system was no longer suppressed by medication, it destroyed the transplanted kidney, but it also eliminated all trace of cancer.

The Holistic Viewpoint

Thomas Edison said, "The physician of the future will give no medicine, but will interest patients in the care of the human frame, in nutrition, and in causes and prevention of illness." Not a physician himself, the great inventor clearly saw that human beings limit the body's natural ability to heal itself by depending too much on drugs.

Although we haven't yet reached that enviable state in which we can do without medications, many in the medical profession now recognize that in treating disease, the whole person must be considered. Rather than focusing only on the diseased part of your body, they treat you mentally and spiritually as well. Thus they are said to practice *holistic medicine*.

Holistic physicians understand that poorly managed stress causes the hypothalamus to shut down the immune system and allows the body to suffer the physical symptoms of anxiety. They see the solution to many diseases as finding a way to prevent the limbic brain from turning on the hypothalamus.

Holistic medicine is nothing new. Rather, it is a modified return to the wisdom of the past. As far back as the days of the Greek healing cult of Asclepius, practitioners used mental imagery to heal. They believed that when the sick experienced a positive event internally, their bodies would heal themselves. Only during the past century have doctors had antibiotics and sophisticated surgical techniques. Before that, physicians knew little even about basic sanitation. Yet they did help patients get well because they inspired them to believe they could be healed. Then the body's natural healing ability achieved the cure.

Holistic doctors do make use of today's sophisticated surgical techniques and medications. But they also treat the whole person by prescribing relaxation, visualization, exercise, and nutrition programs. They are having exciting results.

Dr. O. Carl Simonton, a radiation oncologist, and Stephanie Matthews-Simonton, a psychotherapist, use self-awareness techniques at their Cancer Counseling and Research Center in Fort Worth. They believe that an individual's reaction to stress and other emotional factors can contribute to the onset and progress of cancer. Conversely, a patient can contribute to survival through positive expectations, self-awareness, and self-care. So they teach techniques for learning positive attitudes, relaxation, visualization, goal-setting, pain management, exercise, and building an emotional support system. Patients are helped to visualize the shrinking away of their tumors.

The Simontons make no claims to be miracle workers, but some cancer patients have experienced remissions after other physicians told them they were terminally ill. Others have exceeded their predicted life expectancy and significantly altered the quality of their lives.

Physiological psychologist Jeanne Acterberg-Lawlis, Ph.D., and G. Frank Lawlis, Ph.D., a psychologist at the University of Texas Health-Science Center at Dallas, have used imagery, counseling, and traditional medical care to help patients with many different health problems. They have documented cases of broken bones healing faster and of patients being stabilized even though their diabetes was so rampant they had been told they did not have long to live. Through biofeedback techniques, rheumatoid arthritis patients have reduced pain. Alcoholics and patients suffering from chronic back pain have recovered. Surgical nurse Cornelia Kenner at the University of Texas Health-Science Center–Parkland Hospital Burn Center, has also helped severely burned patients reduce their excruciating pain by using imagery.

Dr. Elmer Green, a physicist on the staff of the Menninger Clinic in Topeka, Kansas, has used biofeedback training to help patients stop bleeding, control temperature, and heal themselves of such usually fatal diseases as Crohn's disease.

Finding the Right Doctor

Although holistic health measures are being increasingly accepted by the medical community, many physicians still refuse to acknowledge that mental techniques can aid in your healing. They may be willing to say that many patients who ''should'' be dead remain alive and even get well for some unexplainable reason. They know the importance of the will to live. Yet they restrict their own therapy to pills and surgery.

Talk to your doctor about holistic medicine. Learn whether he or she will encourage or discourage you in your attempts to use your mind to reduce stress and its effect on your body. If you sense a negative response to holistic techniques, you may want to select a different doctor.

Do not misunderstand me, however. I am *not* telling you that you should stop taking medication prescribed for you. Furthermore, I am *not* saying that cure or improvement is guaranteed through holistic practices. What I am saying is that holistic doctors will use *all* the tools available for healing, including the mind.

Your Goal Sheet

Should you really set a goal to get well when the doctor tells you your disease is chronic or terminal? Of course! Make a long-term goal to get rid of your physical impairment. Then break down your main goal into short-term goals that will allow you to make progress and get positive feedback. If you have been given a medical prediction of doom, you are likely to have either a burning desire to get over your disease or a terrible feeling of depression about your future. What better motivation could you have for committing yourself to using the Five Basic Principles to gain a sense of direction and control?

Here is a typical long-range goal sheet for a cancer patient:

Goal: I will be completely well.

Visualization:
1. I see myself as perfectly calm, radiating health.
2. I see my cancer cells getting weaker. I see my white blood cells as if they were knights in armor, killing off the cancer cells.
3. I picture myself taking part in my hobby, able to enjoy it.

Affirmations:
1. Every day I am getting healthier and healthier.
2. My body has the natural ability to heal itself, and I am helping it do so.
3. I am feeling fine and able to do the things I want to do.

Cognitive Restructuring:
1. Rejectionitis: I will quit telling myself that others do not like me when they don't visit me. I will be grateful for those persons who love me.
2. Negative focus: I will stop letting myself think only of my disease and will replace those thoughts with positive ones about things I intend to do in the future.
3. White-is-black thinking: I will stop predicting that bad

things are happening and train myself to think of good things.

4. Fictional fantasies: I will stop telling myself that cancer is just something I must adjust to and instead cultivate an attitude that I deserve good health.

Acting As If:

1. I will go to alpha six times a day and rest for five minutes before programming for better health.
2. I will learn all I can about my disease so that I can make my visualizations and affirmations more concrete and effective.
3. I will give compliments to five people every day to avoid rejectionitis and keep myself in an extroverted, positive frame of mind.
4. I will take time to read about my hobby.
5. I will use the Blue Dot and Rubber Band techniques to discern when I am thinking negatively and immediately replace those thoughts with affirmations.
6. I will take the prescribed medication.
7. I will tell other people that I am going to get well.

Why Deny the Obvious?

You may be thinking that it is unrealistic to use affirmations such as "I see my body as perfectly well," or to tell other people that you are going to improve when the doctor is predicting otherwise. Obviously when you are with your doctor, you do not deny that you have an ulcer or a heart condition. The point is not to reinforce fears with worry statements and mind chatter and thus hamper your body's ability to function at its best level.

Dorothy, a woman in her fifties with a malicious case of diabetes, made dramatic improvements in her health when she began acting *as if* she were well. Circumstances hadn't been too pleasant for Dorothy. When she returned home from work, her chronically depressed husband, sitting around in his bathrobe, scarcely spoke to her. Dorothy was depressed, too. She kept telling her friends how awful she felt and how blue she was. She also frequently "forgot" to stay on her strictly regulated diet. The result was that her blood sugar skyrocketed time after time. She was spending a lot of time in the hospital.

Then one day a friend brought Dorothy to hear me speak. For the first time, Dorothy learned that many diseases were psychosomatic—real illnesses caused by the mind. She heard me say that by giving in to stress and negative thinking, you can complicate even a disease like diabetes. As soon as she heard that the mind can help overcome stress and allow healing to take place, she set a goal to be well and started acting *as if.* "I feel wonderful. A miracle has happened. I am really okay," she began to tell her friends. Then she set a short-term goal: she would go to her high school's fortieth reunion in her home town. Dorothy had not vacationed for years for fear her diabetes would flare up, so her friends were shocked and skeptical. But Dorothy kept acting *as if* and thinking positively. She went to the reunion, managed to stay on her diet, and had a thoroughly wonderful time. Now the doctor says her condition is stabilized. She hasn't been back to the hospital since she asserted her goal.

Was this a miracle? Dorothy thought it was. "I set a goal of enjoying life. I told my unconscious I felt wonderful. I visualized myself having plenty of energy. And somehow it all happened!" she said.

Dorothy did *not* stop taking her insulin shots or going to the doctor for checkups. She used all the medical expertise available to her, but she added a potent weapon: she enlisted her unconscious to help her by believing and expecting that it *could* help her.

Tips for Working on a Health Goal

• Make your visualizations as detailed as possible. Holistic doctors educate their patients about what is happening to their bodies because of the disease process. Psychologists then help patients draw effective and positive images about how their bodies are healing themselves. They encourage patients to visualize white cells as piranhas or little animated figures with sharp teeth which are eating up cancer cells or as soldiers killing them and pushing them out of the body. Each time they receive chemotherapy, these patients learn to picture their white blood cells getting stronger. They may visualize a shining light that circulates throughout their vascular system.

  You should read all you can about your anatomy and your illness. Then map out the healing process and finally visualize it at alpha. What is happening to your organs, blood vessels, muscles, and bones? What are your body's natural defenses? Use your imagination and literally draw what you would like to see happen. Visualize in color and cheer a little as you watch the cancer cells die!

• Avoid turning your thoughts inward and concentrating on your failing health. Use blue dots to discern gloomy thinking, and hand out compliments to others as a way of forcing your mind to stop dwelling on illness. Seek out humorous TV programs and positive friends.

• Sharpen your sense of expectancy that you are going to be on earth for a long time by making long-range goals to do interesting things. Phil, a businessman who had

had a heart attack, had become so anxiety-ridden that his work was affected. I advised him to pick out a hobby that he could enjoy whenever he had time. Phil had always loved sculpture, so he set a goal of learning how to sculpt. First, he began to read more about the techniques involved. Then he enrolled in a continuing education course at a junior college. With his new interest, he reduced his anxiety. His blood pressure dropped.

If you aren't well enough to begin your hobby, set a goal to take that trip you've always wanted to make or to join a Great Books Club. You can read about these activities in preparation for your future—and send your unconscious a message that you expect to get well.

The Thing about Miracles

I can't emphasize enough that before healing can take place you must demonstrate your belief that you will get well by acting *as if*. Simply put, you must have faith that your unconscious will work to achieve your goals. This advice is not new. The Bible tells us that. When Jesus healed a blind man, a leper, or a paralytic, he frequently told the person, "Your faith has healed you." He told his disciples that if they had faith the size of a tiny mustard seed, they could move mountains.

A lot of people have a hard time with faith. "How can I visualize myself looking perfectly healthy and affirming that I am already well when my last medical exam was worse than the one before?" they demanded.

In such cases, you must just go on fooling your unconscious until it rewards you with faith. I had to do a lot of acting *as if* when I set out to overcome my colitis. I had had this physical condition for years. Doctors had not been able to give me a thing that would make me well. But in attempting to desensitize myself to my phobia, I began to tell myself I was perfectly normal. I began to visualize myself being able to go places and enjoy myself like a healthy person. Almost miraculously I began to have days when I was free of the gripping sensations. Those small successes encouraged me to set a goal and begin to act *as if* I were well. By practicing my Five Basic Principles, I overcame my ailment. I urge you to have faith in them, too.

CHAPTER 13

~~~~~~

Mental Goals: Breaking the Habits of Smoking, Drinking Too Much, and Abusing Drugs

Miss Anderson, my fifth grade teacher, had a dramatic way of proving to her class how hard it was to break bad habits. She would write the word "HABIT" on the blackboard, then erase the "H."

"See, children, taking away the 'H' doesn't get rid of your habit. You've still got 'A BIT' of it left," she said. Then she erased the "A."

"Did that get rid of your habit? No, you've still got a "BIT" of it left," she said. Then, triumphantly, she erased the "B."

"What do you have left now?" she demanded.

"You've still got 'IT,' " we shouted back. Miss Anderson nodded her head.

"Right. Children, never develop a bad habit, because if you do, you will find it almost impossible to break."

Everyone solemnly promised never to learn any bad habits. It would have been nice if I, for one, could have kept that promise. But the problem with habits is that they are sneaky. Most of the time you never realize that an insidious ritual has taken over until it is firmly entrenched in your mind. Then you try your hardest to eliminate it. But just as Miss Anderson said, you can chip away bits and pieces, but you still have "IT," in big, block letters.

Now that you know about my Five Basic Principles, however, you can set a mental goal of breaking any habit you want—from biting your nails to washing your hands every five minutes—and overcome it. This chapter will focus on breaking the habits of smoking, drinking too much, and abusing drugs simply because so many anxious people have these problems. Why? Listen to a group of anxious people and you will hear these statements:

"A cigarette relaxes me in times of stress."

"A good, stiff drink in a bar after work makes all the day's business problems fade away."

"When I'm not up to par, cocaine gets me going again."

All of these statements are true. If you are anxious, you can medicate yourself with a chemical to feel better. You can get rid of your anxiety—*temporarily*. But in the long run, you are only *increasing* your anxiety. Consider these proven facts:

- The nicotine in tobacco acts as a stimulant on the heart and nervous system. When tobacco smoke is inhaled into the lungs, your heart beats faster and your blood pressure is elevated.
- When you drink enough alcohol to have a hangover, you suffer tremulousness, sleep disturbances, and sometimes even epileptiform seizures.
- Cocaine releases the stores of noradrenaline which your body keeps on hand to produce a fight or flight response during emergencies.

Who needs to put anxiety-producing chemicals like these into their bodies? Certainly no one who has panic attacks. Yet psychologists tell us that if you are subject to anxiety, you are just waiting for bad habits like these to come along—simply because you are trying so hard to alleviate your stress. You are like a target at a firing range. Before you know what happened, you are hit with a habit of smoking, drinking too much, or abusing drugs. At best, these habits will only make you feel more anxious. At worst, they can ruin your life or even kill you. Because of cocaine, Steve Howe, the Los Angeles Dodger who was the National League's 1980 rookie of the year, was suspended. A combination of alcohol and drugs killed David Kennedy, Janis Joplin, and Jimi Hendrix. And lung cancer has been tied directly to cigarette smoking.

Addiction—the Catch-22 of Habits

Scientists have another name for habits so dangerous. They call it *addiction.* When you feel nervous, you reach for a cigarette, a cocktail, or a pill. For a little while these body-soothers enable you to forget your nervousness. So you keep on distracting yourself with them. Before you know it, you have trained your unconscious to believe that you don't "feel" right without tobacco, alcohol, or drugs. If so, you have become *psychologically dependent* on them. If you try to eliminate them, you experience strong cravings and you feel you just can't function without your stress-reliever.

If the substance you are using has the potential for making you *physically addicted*, then your body gradually makes a biochemical and physiological adjustment called *tolerance* to its presence. To get the same amount of comfort or euphoria, your body requires more and more of the substance. Eventually it requires enormous amounts for you to feel "normal." If you try to withdraw from it, your body reacts violently. These uncomfortable feelings reduce or eliminate your incentive to quit.

Tobacco, alcohol, and cocaine have all been proven to be both psychologically and physically addictive. But the good news is that addictions are simply habits and your unconscious controls them. That's why I classify such addictions as mental rather than physical problems. By using my Five Basic Principles, you can access your unconscious and train it to help rather than hinder you in breaking addictions. You can break these habits, no matter what Miss Anderson said.

The Five R Preliminaries to Breaking Habits

The first step in breaking habits is to realize that smoking and overindulging in alcohol or drugs *are often symptoms of the disease of thinking negatively*. If you want to eliminate the symptoms, you must cure yourself of the underlying sickness. The same Five R's that I described in Chapter 7 which enabled you to refuse Mr. Negative's calls will also help you break habits:

- *Realize* you may be using your habit to escape the effects of negative thinking.
- *Recognize* that your habit has become a problem.
- *Refuse* to continue the habit.
- *Replace* your habit with something better.
- *Relax* and use the unconscious.

The First R: *Realize* You May Be Using Your Habit to Escape the Effects of Negative Thinking

When I started smoking and drinking, I didn't realize that I took up these habits because I felt pessimistic and cynical. I was in high school, and I didn't like myself very much. By taking up cigarettes and beer, I could be part of the "in" group and feel less inferior. I never once realized that I could have *chosen* to think differently about myself. I just looked for something to escape the bad feelings my twisted thinking brought.

Although alcohol was never a serious problem for me, sometimes I wished that I could stop drinking so much at parties. But when I tried to stop, I no longer felt normal without the drinks and the cigarettes, too. Even though I was saying with my conscious mind that I wanted to quit, my unconscious boss was telling me, "Oh, no! *You* can't stop smoking and drinking."

Years later, when I actually did stop drinking, I made use of the Five Basic Principles. I went into alpha and asked myself why I felt this way and came up with some cognitive awareness. I discovered that I was thinking in fictional fantasies: I told myself I was a person who couldn't do without alcohol in a social situation. I was doing white-is-black thinking by predicting that I could never stop. And most important of all, I was using mistaken identity. I was telling myself I didn't deserve to have relief from this bad habit because of my low self-esteem.

To overcome fictional fantasies and white-is-black thinking, I reminded myself that I had already desensitized myself to my phobia. Of course, I could break another habit! I restructured mistaken identity thinking by going to alpha and affirming that I deserved the healthy and happier lifestyle that I would achieve by giving up alcohol.

The Second R: *Recognize* That Your Habit Has Become a Problem

In Chapter 7 you used the Blue Dot Technique to recognize when Mr. Negative was calling. You already know when you're lighting a cigarette, reaching for a drink, or popping a pill. But you may be telling yourself that these habits have no bad effect on you.

The surgeon general can print the word "cancer" on your package of cigarettes all he wants. You rationalize away the warning by telling yourself that great-grandpa smoked every one of his ninety-nine years. Or you deny the danger by retorting, "I don't want to live forever." But the plain fact is that you have no way of knowing that tobacco will be as harmless to you as it was to your predecessor. And most of us, given the choice, would rather not exit this world by the cancer route. Besides all that, you can't get around the fact that tobacco is a stimulant that can make you more anxious.

It is even easier to deny the bad effect of alcohol and drugs. You read in the newspaper that another well-known personality such as John Belushi has died from pills and booze. "Thank heavens I don't have problems like that," you tell yourself. You really may not. But *recognize* that lots of people are dependent on chemicals without knowing it.

Sarah insisted that her anxiety stemmed from her family problems. Try as she might, she couldn't make her teenaged sons settle down and keep out of trouble. At the same time, she tried to protect them from the fury of their father. Without a doubt, Sarah did need to let go of trying to solve everyone else's problems and fulfill some of her own needs. But she also needed to stop chain smoking and taking four or five stiff drinks every evening to escape her feelings of failure as a mother. Sarah practiced the Five Basic Principles to learn to relax and reprogram her mind. She used alpha to give up cigarettes and cut back on her alcohol. Then her anxiety attacks ended.

My recognition that alcohol was a problem for me came when I heard one of the Mothers Against Drunk Drivers (MADD) tell how her seventeen-year-old daughter's life had been snuffed out by a driver who had gotten drunk at a cocktail party. I knew that whenever I went to a party, I drank enough so that I did and said things that I regretted afterward. Now I saw what I had denied for a long time; I always had to drive myself home after those parties. I could be arrested for DWI. I could lose my license and go to jail. Even worse, I could be responsible for killing someone like this woman's daughter. Even though I didn't see anything morally wrong with alcohol, it just didn't make sense to keep on drinking. I didn't need to add to my stress by wondering if I was going to kill an innocent person because I drank and drove.

The Third R: *Refuse* to Continue the Habit

This R means what it says. You simply stop accepting the offer of a cigarette, a cocktail, or a snort of cocaine.

"If I could refuse, I wouldn't have the habit," you're probably thinking. The first step in refusing, however, is simply making the decision to quit. Make your goal sheet and plan how you will act *as if*. Then resolve to work on your goal.

The Fourth R: *Replace* Your Habit with Something Better

Whenever you attempt to erase a habit, your unconscious is left with a void. If you don't provide a positive habit to replace the bad one, your unconscious will be wide open to the very next anxiety-relieving habit that rolls down the pike. Thus people who stop smoking often start overeating. Recovering alcoholics may start blaming their spouses for their troubles. Former drug abusers may begin chain smoking or become workaholics.

Exercise was the new habit I selected to replace my old ones. I found that the effort required for my new habit eliminated any desire I might have for self-destructive behavior. When I became a runner, I needed every ounce of strength and every cc of pure oxygen I could get. The last thing I would have desired was to reduce my breathing capacity by smoking and my endurance by drinking. Furthermore, I was so proud of being able to run that I no longer craved an escape from myself. I liked myself as I was, and I didn't need a cigarette or a drink to alter my perceptions or to fit in with the crowd.

The Fifth R: *Relax* and Use the Unconscious

To use the unconscious to help you function without chemicals, go to alpha and simply rest in your own secret place. Just relaxing, without trying to program anything, is the best way I know to stop the jittery feeling you sometimes have when you are trying to do without addictive substances. After you have calmed down, then you can program your unconscious to believe that you truly do not want to use these chemicals any more.

Goodbye, Tobacco

During the ten years that I smoked, I tried many times to quit with little success. Then I married Cindy, a non-smoker who let me know she didn't like my dirty, expensive habit. I already had the realization that I needed to quit. Cindy gave me the burning desire to achieve my goal. Although I didn't know how to reprogram my unconscious then, I fortunately stumbled onto using some of the techniques that I have since seen work so effectively for others. I replaced my old habit of smoking with chewing gum. Furthermore, I used affirmations: I told myself that the gum tasted great. It was super, and it satisfied my need for a cigarette. I told myself that chewing gum was the greatest experience I could have. Within three months I no longer craved tobacco. I haven't smoked for thirteen years. And I no longer need to chew gum.

Now that I know the power of visualizations, I realize that I could have fooled my unconscious a lot faster by going to alpha and reprogramming my unconscious. Here is a goal sheet that will help you plan ways to use my Five Basic Principles:

The No Smoking Goal Sheet

Goal: I am completely free of the habit of smoking cigarettes.

Visualizations:
1. I visualize cool, blue air coming in through my nostrils, passing into my mouth and through my esophagus to my lungs. I see my lungs perfectly pink and glowing with good health as they absorb the clean, smoke-free oxygen I send into them.

2. I see myself joyously floating in clouds of dollar bills—the money I have saved by not smoking.
3. Whenever the mental picture of a cigarette presents itself unbidden to my mind, I quickly draw a big red X over it.
4. I picture myself with the people with whom I usually smoke. I use Emotional Transfusion to enjoy myself with them even though I do not have a cigarette in my hand.

Affirmations:
1. I enjoy breathing fresh, clean air.
2. I like being in control of my actions. I can choose to do whatever I like.
3. I like being better able to taste and enjoy my food and having my breath smell good.
4. I like being able to save money by giving up cigarettes.
5. I deserve to be completely free of any addiction.

Cognitive Restructuring:
1. White-is-black thinking: I will stop predicting failure and instead predict success in breaking my habit.
2. Fictional fantasies: I will remember that even though I was a smoker in the past, I am now able to be in control of my actions. I can choose to avoid cigarettes.
3. Mistaken identity: I will stop thinking negatively about myself and build up my self-image so that I can believe that I am worthy of success in breaking my habit.

Acting As If:
1. I will refuse to accept the offer of a cigarette. When I can, I will ask people to refrain from smoking in my presence. The smell of the smoke disgusts me.
2. If I have cravings, I will chew gum, or I will stop what I am doing and practice deep breathing and relaxation at alpha.

3. I will tell everyone I know that I have stopped smoking so that they will be less likely to offer me a cigarette.
4. I will record each day's "attaboys!" on my calendar and frequently review how many days I have gone without smoking.
5. I will accept any compliments I receive for having stopped smoking.

No-Fault Drug and Alcohol Addiction

Anxious people often become addicted to drugs and alcohol through no fault of their own. Delia received a prescription for tranquilizers from a child psychiatrist when she was only ten. She was having stomachaches, a fear of heights, and claustrophobia, and the psychiatrist felt tranquilizers would help her relax. By the time she was sixteen, however, Delia was taking 60 milligrams a day—four times the original dose—and her anxiety was growing worse. When she started to hyperventilate, her family doctor added Seconal, a barbiturate, to her collection of tranquilizers. Delia's mother was worried about her daughter's dependence on drugs. She tried to persuade Delia to give up all the pills. But when Delia tried to stop taking them, she developed muscle spasms in her throat that made her feel as if she were choking. Though she didn't realize it, she was having withdrawal symptoms.

According to a National Institute on Drug Abuse study of addiction to prescription drugs, one in four U.S. women is dependent on mood-altering drugs, as compared with almost one in ten men. Many begin to use tranquilizers, antidepressants, and stimulants on their doctors' advice. They become dependent through no fault of their own.

Delia was luckier than most. At twenty-three she had a sudden burning desire to give up all chemicals because she was pregnant. She didn't want to hurt her baby. She found a doctor who would work with her in gradually cutting back her medication. In conjunction with his therapy she used the Five Basic Principles to desensitize herself to her phobias and to make it easier to give up the pills. Her baby was born healthy. And for the first time in thirteen years, Delia did not have to plan her activities according to the times when she took pills.

Psychologists tell us that abuse of any chemical substance, whether it is alcohol or drugs, is one and the same habit. You can settle your jittery nerves with a cocktail, a sleeping pill, or a tranquilizer. Or you can lift yourself out of the doldrums with cocaine or too many diet pills. The effects may be different, but the habit is the same: you are depending on a chemical to escape your bad moods.

How do you know whether you have inadvertently become physically or psychologically dependent on alcohol or drugs? Answer the following questions which therapists use to determine when someone is in trouble with a chemical substance:

1. Do I experience a meaningful change from the use of alcohol or drugs? Do I drink or take medication to relieve tension, fears, anxieties, or inhibitions?
2. Do I find myself involved increasingly in thoughts about alcohol or drugs? Am I thinking about whether I have enough of these substances when I should be thinking about other things?
3. Are most of my friends heavy drinkers or drug abusers?
4. Has my drinking and use of medication become more secretive, more guarded?
5. Am I drinking or using drugs more often and more heavily than in the past? Am I kidding my-

self that by drinking beer or wine or by using marijuana instead of cocaine I am cutting down? Do I tell myself I am handling my problem because I maintain periods of not drinking or using drugs at all in between binges?

6. When I start drinking alcohol or using drugs, do I end up taking more than I intended? Do I find drunkenness occurring at closer intervals?
7. Have I failed to remember what occurred during a period of drinking or using drugs last night, yesterday, or even a longer period ago?
8. Do I feel guilty, defensive, or angry when someone wants to talk to me about my drinking or use of drugs?
9. Am I sneaking my drinks and my pills?
10. Have I stopped sipping my drinks and instead find myself gulping or tossing them down quickly?
11. Do I lie about my drinking or use of drugs?

The answers to these questions should help you decide whether you have a serious problem. If you do, I strongly urge you to get professional help. But don't feel badly about it. And don't let anyone tell you that once you're a drug or alcohol-dependent person you'll always be one. You can get over both a physical and psychological addiction with professional help. Then, once you have freed your body of the substances, my Five Basic Principles will help you maintain your freedom from them.

I have known many reformed alcoholics and drug abusers who overcame addiction through professional help bolstered by support groups such as Alcoholics Anonymous. Many say, "I'm not glad that I had a problem with alcohol and drugs. But I am glad that because of it I have found a new way of living that is better than I ever could have imagined."

How I Overcame My Drinking Habit

Since I was never an alcoholic, I was able to use the Five Basic Principles to overcome drinking without professional help. You may be able to do the same thing.

First, I wrote out my goal sheet. Then I began programming my unconscious and telling my friends that I had quit drinking. The response was usually a startled, "Oh, I didn't know you had a problem with alcohol." No one could believe I gave it up just because I wanted a better-quality life. That's how brainwashed our society is about alcohol!

At any rate, before long I could go to a party, drink fruit juice or a cola, and have just as good a time as anyone else. I could drive home feeling good about myself. How great it was—no "mornings after" ever again!

I have had no experience with drug abuse, but I know people who have given up their desire to use tranquilizers, marijuana, cocaine, and any number of other harmful chemicals by using the Five Basic Principles.

How do you know whether you can use my techniques alone or whether you need professional help? Try setting your goal and programming yourself for thirty days. If you can go without alcohol or drugs that long, then you can probably continue alone. If you can't, you probably need to make outside help part of your habit-breaking program.

The Drug and Alcohol Goal Sheet

Goal: I am perfectly happy without drinking alcohol and using drugs.

Visualizations:

1. I picture myself looking healthy and relaxed.
2. I see myself removing big clamps that are keeping my arms and legs from moving as I want them to. I see my arteries and veins filled with a sparkling red liquid that represents my blood, which is perfectly free of chemicals.
3. I see my brain as if it were the pistons in a fine-tuned auto. Each piston fires in perfect timing, enabling me to think clearly.
4. I see myself at a party and draw big red X's on the cocktail glasses in everyone's hands.
5. I use Emotional Transfusion to see myself feeling perfectly happy and at ease at a party without a drink in my hand.

Affirmations:

1. I am getting healthier and healthier every day without alcohol and drugs.
2. I like being able to function without any chemical interference to my body.
3. I am free of any desire to drink alcoholic beverages or use drugs.
4. I enjoy being at parties without drinking or getting high.

Cognitive Restructuring:

1. White-is-black thinking: I will stop telling myself I can't quit or that I can't enjoy myself without alcohol and drugs. I will predict success rather than failure in breaking my habits.
2. Fictional fantasies: I will remember that I can choose to do whatever I wish. Though I formerly used alcohol to escape bad moods, I now choose to deal with them in more constructive ways.
3. Mistaken identity: I will remind myself that I have broken other bad habits, such as a phobia or overeating or

overworking. Of course, I will be able to break this one, too. I am worthy of success.

Acting As If:
1. I will refuse offers of drinks or drugs.
2. I will tell everyone I know that I have stopped using alcohol and drugs.
3. I will substitute a good exercise program to attain relaxation rather than using alcohol and drugs.
4. I will do some advance planning rather than depend on alcohol to have a good time at a party. I will learn some jokes to tell and will plan ways I can demonstrate my interest in others rather than worrying about whether I am making a good impression.
5. I will record my "attaboys!" and frequently review them.

Conquer One, Conquer All

As you can see, the two goal sheets I have outlined for breaking the smoking and alcohol/drug habits are somewhat similar. That is because all habits respond in the same way to my Five Basic Principles. If you are an anxious person, you probably have many habits you have developed to cope with your uncomfortable symptoms. I urge you to develop your own goal sheets and use my Five Basic Principles to eliminate behaviors that interfere with your chances to become free of anxiety.

CHAPTER 14

~~~~~~

The Spiritual Goal: The Power within You That You May Not Know You Have

If you have panic attacks, you automatically have a burning desire to work on the physical and mental goals that can bring you relief. But whenever I talk about setting spiritual goals, I find many people shrug their shoulders and say, "That's not for me. I'm just not interested."

If this is how you feel, I can understand. My spiritual life was once completely dormant. Until I recognized that I had a spiritual self, I could not imagine its power to help me reduce anxiety and work on other problems. Once I experienced the peace that my spiritual self brought, I looked back and realized I had been traveling life's highway like a car with a flat tire. I didn't know anything was wrong. I just felt the road was awfully bumpy and my car was laboring hard. I worried because I couldn't find any solutions.

Even if you don't have a burning desire to set a spiritual

goal, I urge you to commit yourself to doing it. When all four of your tires are aired up and your cylinders firing, you can relax and let the overdrive do all the work. You can be free of anxiety.

The Power of the Spiritual Self

The beauty of being in touch with your spiritual self is that it is a way to *tap into a power source that you don't even have to be aware of.* When a doctor told my friend Lane that he would have to lose seventy pounds if he hoped to live long enough to see his grandchildren, Lane began to develop panic symptoms. He had the burning desire to count calories and improve his nutritional habits. But somehow, every evening before he went to bed, he couldn't seem to pass by the refrigerator without falling to temptation. No matter how many times he told himself he wouldn't do it, he opened the refrigerator anyway. As if in a trance he watched his hands dish out a big bowl of ice cream. Then, as if he were powerless to stop, he wolfed down the calorie-laden stuff.

The harder Lane tried to stop his nightly binges, the more anxious he became. At work his heart would pound. He couldn't sleep at night because his heart beat so fast he would have to get up and sit in a chair. His doctor gave him tranquilizers, but they didn't seem to help. Then he started practicing my Five Basic Principles. The relaxation periods at alpha were so wonderful that he began to spend a lot of time at his secret resting place. While there, he felt that he was supported by a force that was not himself—a warm, kind, and loving force that let him know that he was a good and worthy person. Daily he sat and basked in this presence. And then a strange thing happened. When he passed by the refrigerator one night, his hand reached out to start to open the door. But as it did so, a calm but persistent force seemed to stop it in midair. The same loving presence that he felt in his secret resting place swept over him, enabling him to continue to walk right past the refrigerator and go to bed. The same thing happened night after night.

"I lost weight because my spiritual self helped me," Lane told me later. "It also helped me overcome my anxiety. Somehow my spiritual self just took over, even though I never knew I had such a power within me."

Defining Terms

One reason why I had never considered working on a spiritual goal was that I did not know the difference between being religious and being spiritual. I thought these terms were one and the same. Now I know that being religious means knowing *about* the creative power of the universe. Being spiritual means being *of* that universal mind. All my life I had been trained in how to be religious, not spiritual, and I hadn't received much benefit from that.

In fact, a lot of what I learned in my church as a child had a negative effect on me. I memorized Bible verses. I learned that there was a God and a life after death. Somehow I also got the feeling that if you followed a lot of rules and knew about all the dogma and doctrines of a particular church, you would go to heaven after you died. If you didn't, you would go to hell.

Being the nervous, insecure person I was, I knew that I wasn't measuring up to all those rules. I didn't think about it a lot, but down in my unconscious I did negative focusing on my failures. Going to church and learning about dogma, doctrine, and hell actually fed my anxiety.

In fairness, I must admit that some of the Bible verses I

memorized said that the Kingdom of God was within you. Yet I didn't seem to get any training on how to find that inner spirit. I never realized that the power that created the universe was right inside of me, just waiting to help me.

I had heard people talk about the wonderful changes that came about in their lives after a personal contact with God. While I was suffering behind closed doors with agoraphobia, I wanted that contact very badly. I prayed and prayed to God, asking him to stop all the terrible things that were happening to me, but I never felt any peace from any prayers. I never felt any power changing me. It was as if a wall were between me and any God-power that could help. I didn't know how to penetrate that wall.

Once I began to get over my phobia and build my self-esteem, I read a lot of books on positive thinking. In them I discovered that people were able to give up negative thoughts when they had a spiritual source that I didn't have. I saw that this source sustained them during stressful times. So I set my goal to discover my spiritual self. Through meditation combined with prayer, I began working on making this deeper spiritual connection.

The way I did this was to relax and allow myself to look for my spiritual self within *me*, not on the outside, not in a book or a church. And I *did* find that spiritual part of me that everyone has inside. I developed a keen sense of oneness with what I call the spirit of God and which other people call a universal consciousness or a higher power. This oneness has given me a strength and feeling of peace that I never had before. Although the other goals enabled me to overcome my phobia in tangible ways, the spiritual goal eventually led to a transformation experience: *I no longer feared anxiety.* The spiritual goal is the one that ultimately allowed me to love myself and others and find success in life.

What Is the Spiritual Self?

Although I am saying that each of us has a spiritual self, I am not saying that we are gods ourselves. This power of the spirit is a part of us, and yet it is also separate. Every religion points to this truth and has its own way of expressing it. Buddhists find the solution to the problems of sorrow and suffering through seeking an inner experience they can only describe as being enlightened. Hindus teach that man can become one with the Supreme World-Soul, or spirit, through Yoga, the proper discipline of mind and body. They believe this union brings bliss beyond change or pain. In the Bible, the psalmist asks, "Whither shall I go from thy Spirit?" and assures us that the sustaining power of the spirit is with us regardless of the circumstances in which we find ourselves. Jesus said, "The kingdom of God is within you," and promised his followers that when he ascended into heaven, he would send them the Holy Spirit to aid and counsel them.

Every religion, every church, has as a part of its teaching the fact that a spiritual experience can change anxiety into calm, resentment into love, and frustration into peace. It can be a source of power and creativity far beyond anything you can conjure up in your conscious state for reducing stress, breaking habits, and achieving goals to make your life better.

But sadly, people often get so caught up in learning *about* religion that they lose the point of it all. The real goal should be to make contact with this inner spirit and let it make wonderful changes in you.

Goal Sheet to Discover the Spiritual Self

Goal: I will discover my spiritual self.

Visualizations:
I will not attempt to visualize anything; rather, I will go into alpha, still my mind, go to my secret resting place, and relax.

Affirmations:
1. I have a spiritual self that will be a great help to me.
2. I want to discover my spiritual self.

Cognitive Restructuring:
1. White-is-black phenomenon: I will stop predicting that I will never find my spiritual self, or that if I do, it will somehow be inferior and not helpful. Instead, I will open myself to the possibilities that I can find it and it will do wonderful things for me.
2. Fictional fantasies: I will recognize that I have doubts, but that doesn't mean that the spiritual truths don't exist. I will remind myself that these gifts of the spirit are available for me, also.
3. "Should" and "ought" legalisms: I will avoid thinking that I should make the spiritual realities conform to rules I may have learned as a child.
4. Mistaken identity: I will stop telling myself that because of past mistakes I don't deserve to discover my spiritual self.

Acting As If:
1. I will go to alpha three times a day, and before going to my secret resting place I will ask my unconscious to allow me and my spiritual self to come together.
2. I will remain in my secret resting place thirty minutes

a day. If I feel nothing else, I will simply allow myself to enjoy the peace and calmness that comes.
3. I will read books on the spiritual life that appeal to me.

Tips for Achieving Your Spiritual Goal

If you are an atheist and don't believe there is any higher power or universal consciousness or God, you may feel awkward asking your unconscious to bring you together with your spiritual self. Even so, you can discover your spiritual self if you do what your goal sheet says: meditate and act *as if*. Eventually you will fool your unconscious into believing that you really do expect to find your spiritual self. Then, without your having to work to get it, you will receive that wonderful feeling of oneness with a creative power that will change your life.

Here are some tips for making it easier to follow your goal sheet:

- Always find a quiet place behind a locked door when you are meditating so that you won't be disturbed or worry about being disturbed.
- Listen to your unconscious rather than telling it what you want it to do. Many people who believe in prayer don't know that they can stop "putting in orders." Thinking they have to do all the talking, they never simply relax, listen, and discover a new form of communication. If this is a problem for you, try going to your secret resting place at alpha and still your mind. Just rest and enjoy the beauty and quietness there.
- Avoid trying to rush. If your mind is on the clock, it is not likely to be open to receive the spiritual

self. Allow time enough so that you can relax and go deep within yourself.

- Once you have found your spiritual self, maintain daily contact. At this point, you won't have to spend thirty minutes each time you go to alpha working on your spiritual goal. But then, again, you may find that you want to do it. It will be so enjoyable and relaxing that it will be something you desire to do.

How Will I Know When I Find It?

No one can tell another person what it feels like to discover the spiritual self because for each person it is different. All I can say is that you will recognize it when it comes. The effect is a feeling of joy, peace, and quiet exhilaration. Your body feels calmer than it has ever been. You will feel a tremendously creative source of power at work within you.

For Millie, discovery of the spiritual self meant a completely new feeling of being able to handle different relationships. Millie had always felt inferior and insecure. In her late thirties, she developed anxiety, headaches, and indigestion which she felt were caused by her poor relationship with her husband, Peter. Unfortunately, he must have felt insecure, too, because he reduced the stress he felt from his job by taking it out on Millie.

"Peter had to travel a great deal in his work. Whenever I used to meet him at the airport, I always hoped he would greet me with a kiss like I saw other men doing with their wives. Instead, Peter always had a scowl on his face. He either refused to say anything or he started picking on me," said Millie. Feeling rejectionitis, Millie usually ended up by either sulking in return or getting angry and picking a fight. Eventually she developed headaches and a feeling she was going to black out just by going to the airport. She tried practicing the Five Basic Principles, but didn't feel she was making much progress.

"Have you tried setting a spiritual goal?" I asked.

"Oh, Bob, I don't believe in all that foolishness," she said.

"Try it anyway," I advised. So she did, even though she was an agnostic and felt hypocritical in asking her unconscious to help her get in touch with a spiritual self she didn't believe in. But Millie persisted. She read a lot of books about the spiritual life. She spent thirty minutes at her secret resting place each time she went to alpha. Gradually she began to feel a state of happiness that was more than just being calm each time she did this.

"It was very strange what happened," Millie said. "I had become so angry with my husband that I could only think in terms of demanding that he stop using me for a scapegoat. Now I saw that I could change myself in ways that would have an effect on him. I decided to set a goal of having a better relationship with Peter by being accepting of him when he was in a bad mood. I decided that I would be loving and supportive of him no matter what. So I visualized myself meeting his scowls with a smile and affirming that I was a worthy person in my own right, a part of God's creation."

To Millie's surprise, she began to feel this spiritual part of herself taking over on the way to the airport, even though she was driving the car and couldn't be programming herself.

"By the time I met Peter, I was in such a state of euphoria that nothing he did could make me react," she said. Because this spiritual side of herself allowed her to stay calm and loving, her husband's attitude gradually improved. Millie's headaches and feelings of anxiety were gone, too.

"For me, discovery of the spiritual self meant being calm and relaxed, but it was more than that, too. It was feeling different about myself and other people," Millie said.

Once you discover your spiritual self, you may find it hard to describe to another person. You will simply realize you are different from the way you were before. And you will have a new power within to change yourself and ultimately others.

CHAPTER 15

~~~~~~

The Mental and Spiritual Goal: Building Better Relationships

When Fred was promoted to a middle-level executive position by the age of twenty-nine, he was ecstatic. A hard driver who had his sight set on nothing less than the presidency of a major corporation, Fred was determined to outshine all the other young officers. But he drove his staff members too hard. They started to rebel. When Fred's performance rating slipped, he began having insomnia. Sometimes at work his heart would race and he would break into a sweat. Finally, he called me and I explained how he could use the Five Basic Principles to stop his anxiety.

"It's not just these terrible physical feelings that worry me, Bob," he said, and then hesitated. "I get so angry. All those people in the office—sometimes I feel that if I could just . . . well, get rid of them, I'd be okay."

"I know what you mean because I used to feel that way, too," I told him. "I spent a lot of time trying to make people change, and when they wouldn't I got so frustrated I just wanted to kill them."

"I've been doing that, too," Fred said. "And I'm scared. I'm not the type to commit murder, but what if I get carried away?"

"You won't if you make a goal to improve your relationships," I told him. Then I explained how he could break what I call the Poor Relationship Spiral. A lot of anxious people get into this spiral because they are not getting along with someone who is important for them. This stress causes anxiety symptoms which in turn cause distorted thinking as Fred was doing. They blame others for their own shortcomings. Or they use black-is-white thinking. No matter what the other person does or says, they interpret it the wrong way and use it as proof of their negative assumptions.

I convinced Fred that he could get out of the Poor Relationship Spiral by setting a goal. So he wrote out a goal sheet to establish better relationships with his staff. Through *cognitive awareness*, which he developed through practicing the Five Basic Principles, he saw that he was a perfectionist. So he resolved to act *as if* by setting aside time for himself to enjoy sailing once a week and by studying better management techniques to motivate his staff. Through meditation he also gained *spiritual awareness*. With the self-love spiritual awareness brought, he recognized that no matter what his imperfections were, he still deserved the kindnesses he could do for himself. He began to see his staff members in the same way. They were also human beings who deserved happiness—not computer keys he could push to bring up an automatic and perfect response.

Fred's two-barreled mental and spiritual approach to achieving the goal of better relationships freed him from his desire to "get rid of all those people who are causing the problems.'' As his anxiety decreased, his department's productivity increased.

In this chapter I will show you how to set a goal to achieve better relationships with your coworkers, your friends, and your family. Like Fred, you will be able to break the Poor Relationship Spiral and the anxiety that goes along with it.

The Plain Facts about Relationships

If you are presently locked into a Poor Relationship Spiral, you may feel as fearful and despondent as Fred. You've tried your best to change those persons who fling angry words at you or put you down. When that doesn't work, you hurt. You especially resent people who act this way when they are important in your life. You may, like Fred, feel that the only solution is to get rid of them one way or another.

The paradox is that such feelings not only destroy relationships, they make you see yourself in a very bad light. As your self-image sinks lower, you become more anxious.

The first step in breaking this spiral is to realize that no matter what you do, *other people may not change*. But if you can learn to feel better about yourself, others' actions will not have the same impact. *Your true power lies in changing yourself.* I did that through setting a goal to achieve better relationships and becoming more aware cognitively and spiritually.

While I was battling anxiety, my self-image was so poor that I spent most of my time pretending to be someone other than Bob Handly. Without my mask, people might see me as I really was. And they might not like the real me!

Now that I have cognitive and spiritual awareness, I realize that the reason I thought myself so inferior was that I had made mistakes, plenty of them. And I focused negatively on them all the time. I couldn't forgive myself for not being perfect, but I felt that the only way I could be worthy of others' acceptance was to continue to try and accomplish important things. I drove myself so hard trying to live up to these demands I put on myself that I was fatigued to the point of exhaustion. Little wonder that I had poor relationships. As I sank deeper into the spiral, I told myself that the world was a bad place. I listened to all the tragedies I could find on TV and radio to confirm my conclusion. If everyone was against me and the world was all bad, then I was helpless to do anything about it. I was a victim!

If anyone had told me that cognitive and spiritual awareness was the solution, I would have said that person was crazy. Of course, my thinking was straight. Of course, I believed I was worthy. Didn't I have a burning desire to be free of my panic attacks? Didn't I want love rather than rejection from others? Yes, I wanted those things, but I didn't really believe they were possible for me. Why? Because I was such an inferior person. Other people didn't care. And the world was lousy.

But when I started doing cognitive restructuring, I saw how twisted my thinking had become. When I worked on my spiritual goal, I began to accept myself as I really was, with all my imperfections. I no longer needed to look to others to earn forgiveness for my mistakes. Because I was a part of the universal consciousness, and it was all good, then I was all right, too. And I could accept other persons' imperfections and let them be who they really were.

As my wife, my mother, and my business associates saw that I was no longer a threat to their hopes and dreams and that I would be supportive of them, no matter what they did, they became even more loving and open to me. All of my relationships improved.

How Much Do You Love Yourself?

One evening Cindy and I had some friends in to play a trivia game. I noticed that our friends revealed the way they felt about themselves and others by the way they acted when they didn't know the answer to a question they drew. Some would try to reason out the correct response. Others went along with their intuition and said the first thing that popped into their minds, no matter how ridiculous it sounded. But some just wouldn't guess at all. Their feelings of self-worth were so tied into being perfect that they couldn't risk looking foolish by saying the wrong thing. They would rather lose the point entirely than take the risk of guessing wrong and looking silly in the process.

These friends lacked the love of self that would have allowed them to relax in the company of others. They came across as stiff and cold. I am sure that they were also feeling stress as they attempted to hide their feelings of inadequacy from the rest of us.

Do you love yourself enough to accept both the strengths and weaknesses in your personality? Do you care enough about yourself to let change happen to you? You may be the last to know the answer to those questions. To find out, answer yes or no to the following questions.

1. Do you feel at ease talking about yourself to others?
People who don't love themselves answer this question with two extremes. Some say yes, but their idea of talking about themselves is to name-drop or repeat to the point of nausea the story about how they beat out old John at tennis ten years ago. They come across as bores and everyone

avoids them. The result is a further drop in the self-image, which leads to anxiety and more name-dropping. They slide into the spiral.

At the other extreme are those who answer no and make sure that the subject of conversation is always about other people, the weather, their cat, or world affairs. If they allowed themselves to become vulnerable enough so that people knew what they were thinking, someone might see how inferior they are. I call such people lone rangers. They pull their masks tightly over their faces and agree with viewpoints on politics, food, and fun that are totally obnoxious to them. Then, hating those who are "making" them feel inferior or anxious, they are ready to pull out their six-shooters and blast away at the villains who made them feel this way.

Jake was one lone ranger who had joined my Toastmasters club because he got so nervous making the group presentations that his company required. Sure enough, each time he made a speech at Toastmasters, his knees shook and his voice quavered. Furthermore, his speeches were dull. He could see that from the expression on the faces in his audience. One day, I took him aside.

"Look," I said, "your speeches are fine except that you give us nothing but facts and statistics. We want to hear about your feelings, your reactions, your point of view."

"I couldn't do that," Jake argued. "I would feel more nervous than I already do."

"But the audience is as interested in you as a person as it is in the content of your speech. If you don't allow yourself to be somewhat vulnerable, your speech will seem boring."

When it came time for Jake to make the required speech on a controversial subject, he took the risk of removing his mask. Jake chose as his subject the rights of victims of crime. He told about the time he had gotten mugged. When he talked about how angry he felt, everyone in the audience was all ears. Jake could see the interest he was creating. Afterward he received so many congratulations on his speech that he began to see that it was all right for him to be the person he really was.

"Somehow I feel less nervous now," Jake told me. "I feel as if I have some friends in the audience." Jake then tried letting himself be vulnerable at home. In the past he had swallowed his feelings whenever anything his wife and children did pleased or displeased him. Now he began to tell them what he felt, whether it was anger or appreciation. By expressing his true feelings he achieved the deeper intimacy he really wanted with them.

If you talk too little about yourself, check to see whether you are doing *refusing the positives* thinking. Your feelings and viewpoint may be quite different from others', but that doesn't mean they are necessarily inferior. They are what makes you an individual, and people want to know who you really are. Also develop your spiritual awareness that you are a part of creation. Your individuality is acceptable because that is the way you were made.

It's Up to You

2. *Do you feel that other people often take advantage of you?*

Theresa felt her husband, Charles, did that to her. Charles blamed her for everything. "You're a poor manager and you spend too much money. You don't discipline the children. And you never give me the support I need to get a promotion," he complained. Theresa knew she wasn't the cause of all Charles's problems, and she resented his putting the blame on her.

"The reason I have anxiety attacks is because of

Charles," she said. But in working on the Five Basic Principles, she developed enough cognitive awareness to realize that she was playing the victim by doing *my fault* thinking. Whenever Charles put the blame on her, she accepted it. She began to visualize and affirm a better self-image. As she relaxed at alpha, she gained enough spiritual awareness to accept herself—and Charles—as being imperfect but still worthy of love. She then set a goal of improving her relationship with Charles. She affirmed that she was a worthy, loving, strong person. She used Emotional Transfusion to see herself as being calm and happy with Charles as she talked with him in the evenings. She pictured Charles as being happy and calm, too.

One evening Charles complained, "It's no wonder we didn't get invited to join the country club. You're just not the type." But Theresa's spiritual self took over. Instead of reacting with an angry, "You're the one to blame, not me," she found herself saying calmly, "You can say that if you want, but your words cannot hurt me. I know that I am an intelligent person with many likable qualities. I love myself and someday I hope that you can learn to love yourself, too."

Charles reacted in shock. His victim had disappeared from the sacrificial altar. As Theresa continued acting *as if* she were no longer a victim, Charles stopped putting her down. When Theresa quit trying to change Charles and instead changed herself, Charles treated her with more respect. As the hostility in their relationship decreased, they were able to talk about their problems and work toward rational solutions together.

If others are taking advantage of you, check to see whether you, too, are doing *my fault* thinking. Set your goal for a better relationship with the person you feel is taking advantage of you. Work for cognitive and spiritual awareness.

3. Do you treat yourself better or worse than you would a friend or even a stranger?

When you try to comfort persons who have failed in some task, you probably tell them all the things they did right, not wrong. You give them positive feedback about themselves so they can feel better about themselves. Do you do the same thing for yourself? Or do you berate yourself with all the wrong things you did and tell yourself you're just no good?

Rachel was a manager of a group that included several men. They didn't like having a female boss, and they did everything they could to sabotage her. Rachel didn't know how to handle this infighting.

"I know it's because I'm a woman," she often complained bitterly. She sought out other negative people who would take the cue and sympathize noisily with her because underneath it all, she knew she was failing miserably at being a manager. When she began having migraines and other symptoms of anxiety, she started using my Five Basic Principles to overcome them. Through cognitive awareness she realized that she was doing *negative focusing* on the fact that she was female and therefore somehow unable to do what a male manager could do. Deep down, she believed there was a good reason for the men to belittle her.

Rachel then decided that she would treat herself as well as she tried to treat employees who came to her with problems. She would seek out an optimistic, supportive person and express her problem in such a way that she would receive good feedback about herself. She found another female manager and told her, "I have a challenge at the office. I need to establish better management relationships with my men subordinates." Since she didn't complain, the other woman didn't feel called upon to commiserate with her and tell her life was unfair. Instead, she pointed out the good things Rachel was doing and told her about a management course that had helped her. Rachel was so encouraged that she took the course. She set up a system of rewards for accomplishment to which the men responded. At the same time she learned to stand up for herself and let them know who was boss when their performance was out of line. As she did, her migraines began to let up.

When you stop focusing negatively, you can open yourself to receiving positive feedback that will enable you to make changes in yourself.

What to Do about Mistakes

4. When you are feeling less than successful, do you feel better if you can point out a few mistakes other people have made?

When I was changing jobs every year, I used to talk a lot about the mistakes my coworkers made. Somehow I thought that my boss would be less critical of my poor record if I told him how bad everyone else's was. Of course, my finger-pointing only made my boss even less enthusiastic about me. The more jobs I consequently got squeezed out of, the angrier I became at other people. The same dynamics go on in families whose members blame each other for a boring evening, burned toast, or a lack of money.

If you are talking about others' mistakes, you are giving in to *stretch-or-shrink thinking.* You are exaggerating your own inadequacies and trying to compensate for them. At the same time you are shrinking down the good things about yourself so they are practically invisible. Through cognitive restructuring and spiritual awareness, you can accept the fact that everyone makes mistakes, including yourself. You can build yourself up by reminding yourself of the good you do rather than trying to make other people look bad.

5. Do you find it impossible to forgive yourself for past mistakes?

It is amazing how many people say they forgive themselves, that they know that God forgives them and loves them, but still believe they are somehow unforgivable. Let's face it, sometimes we really do make serious mistakes. But that doesn't mean we shouldn't forgive ourselves, as my friend Kay discovered.

Kay had married young, had three babies in a row, and then promptly gotten a divorce. Worried about bills, exhausted by working and caring for the children, Kay sometimes bashed her infant son's head on the floor to make him quit crying. When this son became a teenager, he started getting into serious trouble with the police. Overwhelmed with guilt, Kay felt her son's bad attitude was all her fault. Unable to change him, she developed panic attacks.

Kay tried using the Five Basic Principles, but when she went to her secret resting place, she felt more agitated and nervous than ever. Through cognitive awareness, however, she saw that she was a prime example of *mistaken identity* thinking. Because she had been a child abuser, she was totally unable to see beyond that and believe anything good about herself. She decided to get professional help and to continue to seek spiritual awareness.

Eventually Kay forgave herself. First, she told her son she was sorry for what she had done to him. She let him know she was working on changing herself and that she hoped he would do the same. Then she made positive use of her past mistake. As she gained knowledge in how to deal with child abuse, she volunteered to help other parents in her child abuse support group. She not only found close friendships within the group; she stopped having panic attacks, too.

If you have done something of which you are ashamed, just accept the fact that it happened and stop replaying the scene and the bad feelings over and over again. Make amends if you can. Learn from your experience. Then affirm that you forgive yourself and that God forgives you, too.

What to Do about Others

6. Do you feel that you haven't accomplished what you would have liked because a family member or someone close to you wouldn't let you?

If so, you are doing *white-is-black* thinking. You are measuring your self-worth by what others think of you or how they act toward you. Don't give away your power to other people by letting them make decisions about how you will feel about yourself. Aim for the spiritual awareness that will enable you to love yourself no matter what anyone else says or does. Aim for the confidence to take choices into your own hands.

That's what Bill did after years of blaming his nagging wife, Erika, for his shortcomings. Erika often told Bill, "You never do anything right. You're just plain stupid." She often demonstrated her contempt for him by ridiculing him in front of others. Resentful, Bill retaliated by telling her how unattractive she was.

When Bill developed panic attacks, he began using my Five Basic Principles. He developed enough spiritual awareness to see that he was not the failure Erika made him out to be. He was worthy of self-love and so was Erika. He set a goal of developing a better relationship with Erika. He began to use affirmations about his own worthiness. He used Emotional Transfusion to overcome the resentment he felt against her. By picturing himself doing fun things with Erika and transfusing happy emotions into the scene, he was able to be more relaxed and happy with Erika when he was actually with her.

Bill also realized that to improve his relationship, he needed to demonstrate his attitude of self-acceptance for himself and for Erika. He decided to act *as if* by giving Erika five compliments every day. But what could he compliment her on? Then one day in his visualization he saw that although Erika's clothes were untidy, her legs were quite attractive.

"You know, you've got great legs, Erika," Bill told her while she was reading the newspaper that night. Erika almost dropped the newspaper in shock. But she didn't say anything to him. Later that evening he decided to risk another compliment after he saw her reading to their children at bedtime.

"I think it's important for children to be read to," Bill said. "You're really a good mother." Again Erika said nothing, but she didn't complain about Bill that evening! The strange thing was that the more Bill complimented, the more he found about Erika that was worth complimenting. When Bill changed his white-is-black thinking and risked loving what first seemed to be an unlovable person, both of them changed.

Goal Sheet for a Better Relationship

You may want to set a goal of improving your relationships generally with everyone. Even better, choose one person and aim for improving your relationship with him or her. Here is the way your goal sheet might look.

Goal: I will have a better relationship with _____ .

Visualizations:
1. I see myself with _____ at home, at work. I hear myself talking to him/her in a pleasant tone of voice. I see him/her smiling at me.
2. I see myself touching _____ with warmth and affection, and I see him/her touching me back.
3. I use Emotional Transfusion to develop good feelings toward _____ while we are together.

Affirmations:
1. I am in a loving relationship with _____ .
2. I always respond with love to _____ . I want to support him/her at all times.
3. I and _____ are loving persons. We deserve to receive love from each other.

Cognitive Restructuring:
1. Negative focusing: I will focus on my good points rather than my limitations, so that I can help _____ feel good about himself/herself.
2. Refusing the positives: I will stop refusing to believe that I am able to react with love rather than resentment toward others. I will choose to think positively about myself so that I can better relate to _____ .
3. White-is-black thinking: I will see my own and _____'s actions in the best possible light and affirm the good things in our relationship.
4. Stretch-or-shrink thinking: I will no longer exaggerate my feelings of inadequacy. Instead, I will use spiritual awareness to feel so much self-love that I can be generous in my attitude toward _____ .
5. Mistaken identity: I will forgive myself for mistakes I made in the past and live in the present moment.
6. My fault: I will no longer allow _____ to put the blame

on me for things that are not my fault. I will accept myself as I am.

Acting As If:

1. I will allow myself time to do things that I enjoy rather than forcing myself to spend all my time doing the things that I have thought _____ wanted me to do.
2. I will give _____ five compliments each day.
3. I will seek the advice and counsel of other positive persons if I need it.

Tips for Achieving Your Goal

The hardest part of working to achieve better relationships is acting *as if*. Here are some tips:

• Learn the skills that will help you change. If you recognize your thinking is really distorted, do what Kay did when she overcame the guilt she felt about having been a child abuser. Go to a therapist. Find a support group. Study. Search out the resources that will help you believe in yourself deeply.

Jane's answer was assertiveness training. Jane's elderly mother-in-law made incessant demands on her and put her down with unfair criticism. Jane's husband couldn't see this situation as it was. He insisted that his mother needed Jane's help, even though Jane hyperventilated after every confrontation. Then Jane took an assertiveness training course. Whenever the old lady made a ridiculous demand, Jane said, "I'm not willing to do that." She reinforced her assertiveness and self-love at the alpha level and visualized herself acting firmly. Jane stopped hyperventilating. Strangely, her mother-in-law stopped picking on her.

- Be sure you don't give out unconscious signals of inferiority. Others may actively resist any changes you want to make in your relationship because you are signaling that you are the victim. To change these signals, tell the other person that you have experienced a positive change in your life. You will no longer respond as you have been. Tell him or her that you hope that he/she will also be able to experience a positive change.

- Make the conscious choice to express feelings in a positive way even when you are depressed. Easier said than done, you may say. But you can do it if you meditate and experience more self-love. While you are meditating, look at your alternatives and decide to follow the one that is most positive.

What Will Be the Results?

When you work on a goal of establishing a better relationship with someone, will that other person change? Not necessarily. The important thing about relationship goals is that *you* will change. At the very least, you can expect to have a good effect on those around you. You yourself will become more assertive and loving, more confident and helpful, more serene and less angry.

With more cognitive and spiritual awareness, you will be able to love yourself, regardless of the actions of others. You will no longer feel the anxiety-provoking feelings that you need to rid yourself of from all those others who cause you so much stress. You will end the Poor Relationship Spiral.

CHAPTER 16

Life Plus

The previous six chapters are only a sampling of the goals you can set for yourself. You can fine-tune the goals to fit your specific needs by using cognitive awareness to identify the stressful situations in your life. Then use this awareness about yourself to structure the goals that will benefit you.

As you work on your goals in this way, you may also receive the bonus I did: Life Plus. This was a transformation experience that changed me from an insecure person who worried about everything to one who no longer even considered anxiety as a possibility.

The only way I can describe a transformation experience is to tell you what happened to me. I desensitized myself to my fear of going out in public within a few weeks. Within six months I became more physically fit and free of the bad habits I wanted to end. Even so, my unconscious was telling me I still had to battle against anxiety: "You're not having any panic symptoms now. But you may in the future. You may just suddenly have a panic attack when you're least expecting it." Although I went out to restaurants and parties, I always had the uneasy thought, "Will this be the night all those terrible symptoms return?"

So I continued to set more mental, physical, and spiritual goals. I kept on going into alpha to program my unconscious and to meditate. I acted *as if* I were confident and unafraid.

And suddenly, with no warning, I received my bonus. It was something I couldn't have imagined would ever happen to me. One day Cindy and I were driving down the highway while I listened to a motivational tape. When it shut off, I had a feeling of absolute euphoria! I felt as if I really loved myself! The feeling was so strong I couldn't imagine ever telling myself again that I was inadequate. I loved everyone else, too—all those drivers who were tailgating and cutting in front of us, the clients who were letting me down—absolutely everyone. Nothing anyone ever did would make me angry, impatient, or frustrated again, I thought. When I started describing these wonderful feelings back to Cindy, she cried for happiness!

At first, I thought the wonderful feeling would go away. But it didn't. I was completely transformed. It was like having a "born again" experience, only I called it "Life Plus." The nagging doubts about whether my anxiety would return were gone, simply erased. I was a new person who just didn't have panic symptoms.

Life Plus and the Negatives

Of course, the rough spots in my life didn't all go away after Life Plus. I still had stress, but it was no longer *dis-*

tress, it was *eustress* instead. Let me give you an example. One day as I drove down a thoroughfare, another car driven by a gray-haired lady on a side street ran a stop sign and plowed right into my car. In the eerie silence after the crash, I gingerly moved my body to see that I was all right. Then I got out to look at the smashed fenders. The gray-haired lady was sitting in her car, stunned.

"Are you all right?" I called out. She started to cry.

"I didn't see you coming. Oh, look at your car! It's ruined!" I opened the door and put my arm around her shoulder.

"Now, now, it's going to be all right. We're both okay and that's the important thing," I said.

What was significant about doing that? Before Life Plus, I would have raced out the door of my car shouting how stupid she was! I would have been building up my own stress! Instead, I was comforting her. I wasn't just putting on an act to cover up my resentment. I really did feel concern for this woman. Sure, my car was severely damaged, but I had insurance. It would be inconvenient to get it repaired, but we were both all right. She was another human being, and I wanted to make her feel better.

As it turned out, that wasn't all that happened. When my car was repaired, someone stole it off the body shop's lot before I could pick it up. Several days later, the police informed me they had found my car. It was wrecked and stripped! Back it went to the shop. I was without it for another two months.

This siege of bad luck was a real test of my ability not to answer Mr. Negative's phone calls. Of course, I was angry. Of course, this theft was unfair. I was a victim. I was tempted to think in *fictional fantasies* and tell myself that I was a magnet for bad luck. But because I had Life Plus, I didn't fall into this temptation. I did some cognitive restructuring and reminded myself that overall my life was a wonderful success. I didn't have to dwell on the few drawbacks it held.

It would also have been easy to slip back into my old *white-is-black* thinking and predict, "Bad luck comes in threes. What's next?" Instead, I deliberately chose to tell myself that the worst would soon be over. I would have my car back. Besides, all this bad luck proved to me that I could retain my new positive attitudes even when times were tough.

The result was that my stress became eustress because my body didn't remain at the arousal state continuously. I had periods of calm when it could return to normal in between the times of crisis.

How to Get Life Plus

Will you ever be able to achieve Life Plus? Only if you accept the "new you" that you are creating by goal-setting. You may have stopped smoking or drinking, become physically fit, or improved your relationships. But if you have been nervous and insecure all your life, you may not feel comfortable with the "new you."

Roxanne had just that problem. Herself a perfectionist, Roxanne had always expected her two teenage sons to be the most popular in their class. Her house had to be spotless and decorated like a picture in *Better Homes and Gardens*. Then one day her tidy world fell apart: her husband divorced her. Roxanne went into depression, and so did her sons. The oldest, Lloyd, committed suicide. Then Roxanne had grief and self-blame to overcome as well as her habit of expecting perfection of herself and others.

Roxanne went to a psychologist to overcome her depression. He helped her understand that Lloyd's choice to commit suicide was his own, not hers. She learned new ways of communicating with her other son, Steve, so that the two of them could discuss their feelings openly. Roxanne knew that this new way of relating to Steve was absolutely necessary as a step toward helping him maintain his mental health. But she found it hard to accept the new Roxanne. She began to suffer panic attacks.

"I know how to communicate with Steve. And I want to communicate with him. But the old me still wants to do negative focusing. In the back of my mind I am still the mother who failed because her son committed suicide. I just can't accept that I'm not guilty," she told me.

Roxanne used the Five Basic Principles to overcome her panic attacks. She spent a lot of time at the alpha level programming her unconscious and also meditating. Eventually, Life Plus "just happened" to her, too. With it came the self-forgiveness she hadn't been able to achieve. Afterward she was also able to communicate even more freely with Steve and to love him as he was rather than insist he live up to an impossible ideal. Most important of all, she was able to be kind to herself. Roxanne developed a new and exciting career for herself which included helping other depressed people. "The first step toward getting over depression is to make the choice that you're going to change. The second is to accept yourself once you have changed and to go with the new you," she tells others.

The Movie Called Life

I realize that it is easier for me to tell you to accept the new you than for you to do it. But I can tell you a way that will help. Pretend that you are both the director and the star of your own movie. It's a four-star production titled *The Absolutely Successful, Panic-Free, Self-Fulfilled Life*. Then visualize yourself performing on the biggest movie screen you ever saw. See yourself living in a loving, successful way. If you don't like what you see, then take the director's role and change the script. Set a new goal for a better self-image. Then use the Five Basic Principles to make it happen in your life. You can make your movie turn out any way you wish because you are both the star and the director.

This is just one more way you can make use of your unconscious boss. If your visualizations are vivid enough, if you continue to act *as if*, your unconscious will reward you with the feeling that the new you is just you . . . you as you naturally are.

I am convinced that as each of us learns to change himself or herself through using my Five Basic Principles, we are changing the world. You can't work on a spiritual goal as I have without coming to the realization that all of our minds somehow communicate with each other. As one of us overcomes negative thinking and anxiety and begins to project positive thinking, self-confidence, peace, and love, others are influenced to become more positive. The results can spread like the red, blue, green, and gold sparks that fill the skies when one small rocket is lit on the Fourth of July. The whole universe can change. You can make that movie titled *The Absolutely Successful, Panic-Free, Self-Fulfilled Life* a reality for many others.

It's Up to You

Have I convinced you that you can be free of panic attacks, negative thinking, a poor self-image, physical problems, troubled relationships, and bad habits that stem from thinking about yourself in the wrong way? I sincerely hope so. The Five Basic Principles are not just a theory; they are a practical approach to dealing with all these kinds of irrational thinking and will help you experience real change.

If you program your unconscious to replace your old negative tapes with new productive ones, you can produce a movie of yourself that will be a delight for you and everyone else. You will have Life Plus, an entirely new power in your life to make you into a new person. You can have this if you want it. I know, because it happened to me.

BIBLIOGRAPHY AND
SUGGESTED READINGS

Acterberg-Lawlis, Jeanne, Ph.D. *Bridges of the Body Mind.* Champaign, Ill.: Institute for Personality and Ability Testing, Inc., 1980.

Burns, David D., M.D. *Feeling Good.* New York: New American Library, Inc., Signet Books, 1981.

Cousins, Norman. *Anatomy of an Illness.* New York: Bantam Books, 1981.

Fensterheim, Herbert, Ph.D., and Baer, Jean. *Don't Say Yes When You Want to Say No.* New York: Dell Publishing Co., 1978.

Fensterheim, Herbert, Ph.D., and Baer, Jean. *Stop Running Scared!* New York: Dell Publishing Co., 1977.

Glasser, Ronald. *The Body Is the Hero.* New York: Random House, 1976.

Guzman, Emiliano. *Mind Control.* Laredo, Texas: Institute of Psychorientology, Inc., 1972.

Hill, Napoleon. *Think and Grow Rich.* New York: Fawcett Press, 1960.

Leonard, Jon N., Hofer, J.L., and Pritikin, N. *Live Longer Now.* New York: Grosset & Dunlap, 1974.

Maltz, Maxwell, M.D. *Psychocybernetics.* New York: Prentice Hall, 1960.

McKnight, Harry. *Silva Mind Control through Psychorientology.* Laredo, Texas: Institute of Psychorientology, Inc., 1972.

Morehouse, Laurence E., Ph.D., and Gross, Leonard. *Total Fitness in 30 Minutes a Week.* New York: Simon & Schuster Pocket Books, 1975.

Peale, Norman Vincent. *Dynamic Imaging.* Old Tappan, N. J.: Fleming H. Revell, 1982.

Silva, José, and Miele, Philip. *The Silva Mind Control Method.* New York: Simon & Schuster Pocket Books, 1977.

Simonton, O. Carl, M.D., and Matthews-Simonton, Stephanie. *Getting Well Again.* New York: Bantam Books, 1980.

Smith, Manuel, Ph.D. *When I Say No, I Feel Guilty.* New York: Bantam Books, 1975.

INDEX

A

Acterberg-Lawlis, Jeanne, 189

Acting *as if* technique
application of, 128, 155, 157–158, 161, 164, 177–178, 180, 192, 206–207, 212, 218–219, 230, 237
effectiveness of, 114–116
procedure for, 117–118
reasons for avoiding, 122–124
tips for using, 120–122
use of, for treating panic attacks, 42

Addiction, 199–200

Adrenaline, 21, 37, 38, 130, 150
and agoraphobia, 19

Aerobic exercising, 163

Affirmations
applications of, 119, 122, 154, 157, 160, 164, 177, 179, 191, 192, 205, 206, 211, 218, 236
developing, 84
and Emotional Transfusions, 84–89
functioning of, 73–75
importance of, 80–83
taking control of, 75–80
technique of, 156
as tool, 112
use of positive thinking in, 84

use of, to change self-image, 71–72, 89
use of, to reprogram unconscious mind, 49–51
use of, to treat panic attacks, 42

Agoraphobia, 8, 13, 28–29
definition of, 29

"Ain't it awful" game, 121

Alarm stage, of "fight or flight" response, 21, 150

Alcohol, 198
addictiveness of, 199–200
and calorie counting, 176
harmful effects of, 202–203
no-fault addiction to, 207–210

Alcoholics Anonymous, 210

Alcoholism, relationship between phobias and, 5–6

Alive magazine, 76

Alpha Script, 63–66, 71, 77

Alpha state, 49, 51–52, 56, 57, 182, 230, 240
experiencing, 58–59
feelings while in, 66–69
and goal setting, 142
methods of achieving, 59–66, 69–70
and reprogramming of the unconscious mind, 108–110, 118

Imipramine, use of, to treat
	panic attacks, 23
Immune system, and stress, 22,
	187
Immunosuppressive drugs, 187
Incest victims, development of
	Post Traumatic Stress Dis-
	orders in, 33–34
Inderal, use of, to treat panic
	disorders, 24
Inferiority
	dealing with feelings of, 238
	feelings of, and panic, 7
Ingram, Robert, 14
Irrational fears, as cause of
	stress, 33–34
Irrational thinking, avoiding,
	155.
	See also Negative thinking;
	Positive thinking

J
James, William, 81
Jogging, 162
Johnson & Johnson, 159
Joplin, Janis, 199

K
Keller, Helen, 93
Kennedy, David, 199
Kenner, Cornelia, 189
Klein, Dr. Donald, 23

L
Lawlis, G. Frank, 189
Learning, laws of, 116–117
Librium, 23
Life Plus, 14–15, 239–245
	achievement of, 242–243
Limbic system, 150, 151
Lloyd, Chris Evert, 181
Lung cancer, and smoking, 199

M
Maltz, Maxwell, 39
Matthews-Simonton, Stephanie,
	189
Medications
	no-fault addiction to, 207–210
	use of, in treating panic disor-
	ders, 23–25
Mental dysfunction, 150–151
Mental goals, achievement of,
	197–212
Mental imagery, and disease
	control, 188, 189
Migraine headaches, 5, 151
Minerals, 172
Mistaken identity, dealing with,
	99–100, 155, 157, 161,
	164, 177, 206, 211–212,
	218, 233, 236
Mistakes, effect of making, on
	self-image, 100–101
Mitral valve prolapse, 19, 20
Monoamine oxidase (MAO), use
	of, to treat panic attacks, 23
Mothers Against Drunk Drivers
	(MADD), 203
Muscle reactors, 22
"My fault" thinking, dealing
	with, 100, 102, 103, 230,
	236–237

N
Nardil, use of, to treat panic at-
	tacks, 23
National Fitness Foundation, 163
National Institute on Drug
	Abuse, 207
Navratilova, Martina, 181
Neff, Pauline, 26–27, 139
Negative focus. See also Nega-
	tive thinking
	dealing with, 95, 102, 104–
	105, 154, 180, 186, 191,
	231, 236
Negative learning process, 115

About the Author

Thousands attend Robert and Jane Handly's Life Plus seminars. They have appeared on such shows as "Donahue" and "Nightline." They live in Dallas, Texas.

Dallas-based writer Pauline Neff has collaborated with the Handly's on their previous books.

If you would like more information about Life Plus programs, please contact Life Plus, 7353 Lane Park Court, Dallas, TX 75225, (214) 363-1591.